Rough Passage

Rough Passage

Commander R. D. Graham

and

The Adventure of the Faeroe Islands
M. Helen Graham

GRANADA
London Toronto Sydney New York

Granada Publishing Limited
8 Grafton Street, London W1X 3LA

First published 1936
This edition published by Granada Publishing 1984

British Library Cataloguing in Publication Data

Graham, R. D.
  Rough passage.
  1. Emanuel (*Ship*)   2. Voyages and travel
  I. Title
  910.4'5   G463

ISBN 0-246-12311-7

Printed in Great Britain by
Billing & Sons Ltd., Worcester

CONTENTS

MAPS

INTRODUCTION

In this book is described one of the most remarkable and adventurous small-boat voyages of modern times.

Emanuel is a tiny cutter yacht with a length of 30 feet overall and a beam of $8\frac{1}{2}$ feet. On 19th May 1934, with her owner, Commander Graham, as her sole crew, she left Falmouth bound for the south-west coast of Ireland and thence to St. John's, Newfoundland. On the voyage she had fair winds and good weather varied by gales of short duration, and, towards the end, extreme cold and the sight of icebergs. After her arrival at St. John's, Commander Graham cruised single-handed on the coasts of Newfoundland and Labrador, visiting many creeks as far as Hamilton Inlet.

He became seriously ill from an obscure form of blood-poisoning. For two months he was in bed in the Mission hospital at Cartwright and afterwards at St. Anthony's. When he arrived back in St. John's at the end of October it was bitterly cold, and ice was forming in the shallow water along the shore. The long delay set him a difficult problem. He was still far from well. To lay the yacht up for the winter and return by steamer would be expensive. To sail for the United States would mean a cold and perilous passage in the neighbourhood of land. He decided to get into the warm current of the Gulf Stream as soon as possible and to sail for Bermuda. On the passage heavy gales tested man and boat nearly to the limit. The boom was smashed, and most of the sails and gear were damaged. But the well-tested gaff rig can always be repaired in some sort, provided that the mast stands and that there is sea room. He spent the winter in Bermuda and completely recovered his health.

A friend in Bermuda volunteered to sail home with him. They left for the Azores on 24th April 1935 and arrived in Horta, Fayal, after a passage of eighteen days. Another passage of eighteen days brought them to Scilly.

Commander Graham was awarded the Challenge Cup of the Royal Cruising Club for the voyage from Falmouth to Newfoundland and Labrador. Lest anyone should regard it as a rash adventure, the remarks of the judge who made the award are repeated here: 'The news that *Emanuel* had been sailed single-handed from England to Newfoundland at first caused some misgiving. The Club is for the encouragement of good seamanship and legitimate enterprise, but recklessness is not regarded with favour. But Commander Graham had proved himself and his vessel in cruises to Spain, the Faeroe Islands, and elsewhere. I am satisfied that, having failed to find a companion, he was justified in sailing alone if he wished to do so, and that the voyage was undertaken with adequate knowledge and solely for the love of adventure at sea.'

CLAUD WORTH

ROUGH PASSAGE

Being the Narrative of a Single-handed Voyage
to Newfoundland, Labrador, and Bermuda in
the Seven-ton Yacht *Emanuel* and the subsequent Return to England with a Soldier Crew

BY

COMMANDER R. D. GRAHAM

CHAPTER I

THE SHIP

SINCE my return home, many friends have advised me to write a book describing my experiences on my recent single-handed voyage across the Atlantic to Newfoundland, Labrador, and Bermuda. The labour of doing so is considerable, but it is being undertaken in the hope that it will contribute to the expense of fitting out for the next one.

I have never written a book before, and do not know much about the way to go about it. Perhaps there are schools where one can be taught. There are several volumes of voyages about the house, and I have glanced at them to see if there is any conventional gambit. The result has been very muddling. It seems I had better just go straight ahead and try to tell my story as simply as possible without attempting literary flourishes.

I think it will be of interest to other yachtsmen, and I therefore propose writing as candidly as possible without exaggerations for the sake of making a story.

Other writers are remarkably reticent about how they felt and what they thought during their voyages. This is one of the things one feels one wants to know when reading their books.

There will be a few adventures to describe. Stefansson, the great Arctic explorer, has made some excellent remarks on this subject. Adventures are usually due to mismanagement or to taking undue risks, and are things to be ashamed of.

It is impossible to write intelligibly about ships and the sea without using some technical terms.

Among the many questions put to me on the other side of the Atlantic was: 'What are you doing this for?' There seems no reason why I should not answer it. During the winter of 1933–34 business worries accumulated to such an extent as to affect my health. Not being able to afford a world cruise in a luxury liner, I decided to go in my own ship to some place beyond the reach of telephone and telegraph wires.

By chance, the previous autumn, I had listened in to a broadcast talk on Newfoundland and Labrador by my relative, Sir Wilfred Grenfell. It was his enthusiastic descriptions that first gave me the idea. Anywhere on this side of the Atlantic would have been too close to a telegraph office. There might have been telegrams from home asking what to spray the apples with, or where to market the strawberries.

This reminds me to put on record that it is my wife who is the real hero, or rather heroine, of the affair, since it was due to her agreeing to stop at home and look after the farm that my voyage was possible.

Since my return home many very flattering remarks have been made to me, when my tongue has had to be put into my cheek; because one does not really have to be very brave to make a long voyage in a small yacht. I, myself, am constitutionally rather timid, though with increasing years I have learned to some extent to manage my timidity. One waits for a spell of fine weather before putting to sea. Then, with the sun shining and the blue sea ruffled by a light wind, the yacht glides comfortably along, and it is easy enough to be bold. A day or two later the weather may have changed and it may be blowing a gale, but then one is sufficiently far from land for it to be more dangerous to run back than to continue. One can be as frightened as one likes and must just put up with it.

It is a number of years ago now that, when visiting Mr. Anderson's yacht-yard at Penarth to arrange for the hire of a boat, I saw a vessel under construction. The frames were in place, but the planking had not been begun. A fine, able craft she would be, and the enclosing shed exaggerated her size. Some two years later, in 1928, I saw her again, completed but not fitted out. In the meantime the family mansion had been sold and I had cash in the bank. Knowing full well that this would never occur again, I shut my eyes to the grotesque extravagance and decided to buy her.

A name had to be found for her. She would naturally be registered at my home town of Bridgwater in Somerset, and it seemed fitting that she should be called after some old ship sailing from this once flourishing seaport. On looking up the maritime history of Somerset, I found that Bridgwater had sent a ship named *Emanuel* to join Frobisher's third expedition to Baffin Land in 1578. Accordingly, my ship was christened *Emanuel*. It seemed rather a strange sound at first, but before long she grew into her name, and it now seems the most natural name in the world for a yacht.

There is a curious story about the old *Emanuel*. On the return home she became separated from the rest of the squadron, and between Greenland and Ireland she reported land. There is a circumstantial account by one Thomas Wigar, a passenger, recorded in Hakluyt, stating how they sailed along the land for twenty-five leagues and that it appeared to contain two harbours. Soundings in the nineteenth century give no indication of a sunken island, and it was probably ice that they saw.

My *Emanuel* is a cutter-rigged yacht of seven-ton Thames measurement. She is thirty feet over all, twenty-five feet on the water-line, and has a beam of eight feet six inches and a draught of five feet. Her rounded bow sweeps aft with very pronounced sheer to the short counter. Her freeboard is twenty-four inches. Her deep and fairly straight iron keel weighs thirty hundred-weight, and about two tons of scrap-iron ballast is packed under the floor-boards. Above water the chief feature of her design is the cabin top, which is carried right out to the sides of the ship. This, apart from the increased accommodation below, gives her an enormous reserve of stability and also provides stowage space for the dinghy.

Abaft the cabin is the cockpit or steering-well, the surrounding space being utilised for lockers. The cockpit is not water-tight, so that any water entering it eventually drains down into the bilge. It is small, so that it can be flooded several times without endangering the ship. I never found any danger from it not being water-tight until the voyage from St. John's to Bermuda.

The opening to the cabin can be covered by a sliding hatch and by two small doors. These doors are fitted with louvres to allow ventilation. Splashes may find their way down below, but no solid water. Solid water, by the way, sounds a contradictory expression, but sailors know the term well enough. At the fore end of the cockpit is a recess holding a compass which can be illuminated from the cabin. Another compass is carried on the cabin top.

Below, the accommodation consists of the main cabin with five feet four inches headroom. Being short, I can very nearly stand upright. On each side of the flap-table is the usual settee. In the forward starboard corner is a wardrobe, and on the opposite side a bookcase, both with drawers underneath. In the starboard after-corner is an oilskin locker built around a water tank holding fourteen gallons. On the port side, aft, is the galley, consisting of a Primus stove on gimbals, with plate-rack and small drawers above and a space for cooking utensils underneath.

Separated from the main cabin by a sliding door is the fore cabin, with good kneeling head-room, and containing a full-length bunk on each side. On a long voyage all this space is utilised for spare sails, food, &c. Another door gives access to the forecastle, which contains the lamps, a bucket lavatory, and the anchor chain.

Such was my home for over a year, and very comfortable I found it in fine weather.

CHAPTER II

OCEAN CRUISING

OCEAN cruising in a small yacht is not the hazardous occupation that many people suppose. I am not concerned to argue that there is no risk. There is some, about the same as in hunting or flying, but I am anxious to avoid the charge of foolhardiness and rashness. The sea is not yet tamed, and my ship is subject to its perils as much as others passing on their lawful occasions. It is a matter of some interest to consider more closely exactly what these perils consist of at the present day, and to compare their effects on big and little ships.

Probably the chief danger is collision. Here *Emanuel* scores, as she is such a tiny mark to hit, and she never sails so fast but that it is an easy matter to avoid another ship. Steamer traffic is now mostly confined to definite lanes, which one naturally avoids. It is only after sailing for day after day and week after week without sighting anything that one realises the immensity and the loneliness of the oceans. The risk of running into anything seemed so utterly remote that it was not even worth while to carry lights at night. In coastal cruising, of course, the risk is much greater, and it can be very agitating to lie becalmed in a fog listening helplessly to the gradually increasing roar of fog syrens.

Fire is the next most important danger. In a little ship no serious fire could take hold before it was noticed and extinguished, except where there is an engine, and thus danger from petrol. Normally no petrol is carried on board *Emanuel*, but, in Newfoundland, the paraffin was unsatisfactory in the Primus stoves, and petrol had to be substituted. I was extremely careful, and no accident resulted. Before leaving Bermuda my companion installed a petrol vapour lamp. The two-gallon storage can for this was carried on deck in the dinghy.

Some years back we had a scare of fire. A saucepan half-filled with olive oil was being used for deep frying. It was put on the stove and half-forgotten. My daughter remembered it and lifted the lid, whereupon the whole affair burst into flames. With great presence of mind she seized the handle and flung the saucepan with its contents into the cockpit. The flames went out, though the ensuing mess was rather tragic.

Ships may spring leaks through straining their hulls or other causes. Recent examples are the *Trevessa* and the *Vestris*. In a heavy sea the structure of a ship is exposed to very great strains. The bow and stern may be supported by the crests of waves, while the midship part, bridging the hollow between them, is insufficiently buoyed up. Torpedo-boat destroyers are very long and narrow ships. I served in one in 1908. As the waves passed one could feel the iron deck buckling and stretching as the whole ship bent.

The galleys of classical times were also long and narrow. Greek writers do not comment much on the size of the waves, but express their fear of the 'hollow' seas. Evidently their ships were liable to strain their hulls.

The smaller the ship the stronger, relatively, is her hull. A well-designed and properly constructed yacht can easily bear the strain of being supported by the water at one part and unsupported at another. Long, narrow overhangs are a danger, however, and there is a case on record in recent years of a yacht crossing the Bay of Biscay and being caught in a gale. Her stern became strained, so that she developed a dangerous leak and only just reached port in time.

There is more chance of locating and repairing a leak in a small ship, though, of course, the danger is much more immediate, since a very small leak would quickly endanger a craft of *Emanuel*'s size.

Ships are sometimes lost through seas breaking over them and tearing open hatchways and doors, or even breaking in the decks. If these cannot be repaired and made water-tight the ship will sink.

The smaller the ship the more buoyantly she rides over the waves and the less water falls on board, though, of course, she is much less heavily built and less able to withstand the shock. In a heavy gale the crests of the waves break with alarming noise and force over the vessel, jarring the whole fabric. *Emanuel* is not an especially heavily built ship, and there were times when I thought that it was impossible that her hull could withstand the shocks that it was receiving. Her sides would give quite noticeably. Very possibly it was due to this elasticity that she never suffered any structural damage.

One reads in the newspapers of liners reaching port with boats washed away, bridges wrecked, &c. This is due to their speed. Imagine a large ship steaming, say, twenty knots against the wind. Her bows pitch beneath the top of an oncoming wave, and a mass of water falls on board. The water has no lateral motion, and suddenly meets a solid object moving at twenty miles an hour. The effect is almost comparable to a motor-car running into a brick wall. A small ship has time to pitch several times as the wave approaches, and so adjusts her position to the slope of the water. Comparatively little comes on board. She will be moving only very slowly through the seas. Such water as falls on deck swills harmlessly about without breaking things up.

The actual breaking crests of the waves are a different matter altogether. In an ordinary summer gale these are probably not more than eighteen inches or two feet in height. They give a heavy splash, but there is no real vice in them. In the full fury of a winter storm the top four or five feet of the wave may actually break, and there is a surprising force in such a mass of tumbling water. Perhaps once in every hour such a crest may actually break against the ship, and the smaller she is the more disastrous may be the effect. I do not think that *Emanuel* was ever in danger of being rolled right over, though, as I have mentioned above, I feared for her hull.

How to manage about sleep when single-handed is one of the questions that is frequently asked. When the wind is before the beam the sails can be trimmed and the helm lashed so that the ship will sail her approximate course without attention. One can go below, and sleep on the lee bunk, fully dressed, of course, so as to be ready to spring up at a moment's notice. The ship will naturally be under easy canvas. If the wind increases the ship automatically comes head to wind. The sails shake, and the vessel becomes upright, so that one wakes at once. Sudden squalls are not frequent in mid-ocean, and one knows the sort of weather in which they are likely to occur.

If the wind goes very light the ship will turn

away from it and may gybe. Since the wind is light the gybe will not be dangerous. My usual practice is to trim the sheets and lash the helm so as to get the yacht to sail as near her proper course as possible. An occasional glance at the compass shows how she is actually steering, and every four hours the average course is noted in the log-book. I would be quite satisfied if the average course was within two points ($22\frac{1}{2}$ degrees) of the correct one. Very little distance is lost by such a deviation.

If the wind is abaft the beam and the mainsail is set the ship will not look after herself without some attention. Sometimes, with spinnaker set she will steer herself for ten or twenty minutes with a line round the tiller, but she is apt to wander off from time to time and get one of the sails aback. One can usually feel from the cabin by the motion what she is doing, and attend to the tiller in time to save a gybe. Sometimes she will not steer herself at all with the wind aft; it probably depends on the direction of the underlying swell. When the wind was light I would sometimes keep watch for thirty-six hours at a time, most of it below in the cabin cooking meals or sitting on the table watching the compass and perhaps listening to the wireless. By the end of such a period conditions would probably have changed; if not, the mainsail would be lowered, and the ship would continue sailing more or less on her course under jib and staysail.

She will not thus sail directly before the wind, but goes along with it on her quarter. Occasionally she may shift the wind from one quarter to the other, altering her course eight points. I shall tell later how my ship found Bermuda for herself, since it was due to such an unpremeditated alteration of course that I escaped sailing past out of sight of the island.

One keeps track of one's position by calculations from the course steered and the distance sailed. The latter is measured by a patent log, which consists of a small propeller trailing astern on the end of a rope, and which turns an instrument akin to the speedometer of a car. Whenever opportunity occurs observations of the sun are taken to correct the calculated or dead-reckoning position. On my first voyage I found the dead-reckoning positions surprisingly accurate, usually being within ten or fifteen miles of the observed ones. I think the greatest error was on the day before I sighted Newfoundland, when sights showed that I was twenty-six miles farther off than I had supposed. On my passage to Bermuda, when for perhaps five or six days at a time it was too cloudy or too rough to take sights, my positions were wildly wrong. On one occasion I found myself a hundred miles to the westward, though this was doubtless due to the current of the Gulf Stream; and on making Bermuda my ship was eighty miles ahead of the reckoning.

It is very much more easy to observe the latitude than the longitude. The former is found by a sight at noon when the height of the sun is nearly stationary for several minutes. Longitude requires a sight in the morning or afternoon when the sun is rising or falling rapidly. The difference is comparable to shooting a bird sitting or on the wing. As well as the sun an observation requires a view of the horizon. In bad weather it is only when the yacht is on the top of a wave that such a view is possible, and then the horizon may be obscured by the crest of a nearby wave. Two hands are required to manipulate a sextant, and the violent motion makes it very difficult to hold oneself steady, to say nothing of the spray which is likely to deluge the instrument at any moment. In seriously bad weather I found it altogether impossible to get longitude sights, while those for latitude were mostly in the nature of a guess. But the oceans are wide, and it is only on approaching land that one's position becomes important.

To find one's longitude it is also necessary to know Greenwich time. In latitude $50°$ an error of one minute of time makes an error of nine miles in the position. Nearer the equator the positional error is rather more. Big ships carry chronometers, which are merely specially accurate clocks. *Emanuel* depended on wireless time-signals and an ordinary watch. I reckoned on picking up

American stations in plenty of time before making land. Unfortunately, I was not able to obtain a list of stations with their programmes before starting. How I actually made my landfalls will appear later.

Claud Worth gives the maximum sustained speed for a normal cruising yacht as $1.4\sqrt{\text{water-line}}$. For *Emanuel* this works out as seven knots, and is about right; but to obtain this speed entails really hard driving, much harder than one can attempt in a small craft on an ocean passage, even with a strong crew. One would be afraid to put the necessary strain on the gear and hull. Also, in the open ocean, by the time the wind is blowing strongly enough to sail at seven knots there will be a big enough sea to make such a speed too uncomfortable if not actually dangerous.

Emanuel's best days' runs were 147 and 140 miles on two successive days between Bermuda and the Azores. She was running before a fresh westerly wind, averaging about six knots; but her effective speed is about half that. This, or about seventy-two miles a day, was the average from Bantry to St. John's. The best day's run on that passage was 112 miles, and on five occasions it exceeded 100 miles. Between St. John's and Bermuda, a distance of 1,072 miles, the average was two knots, or forty-seven miles a day.

Between Bermuda and the Azores we encountered very favourable winds, and averaged 107 miles a day for seventeen days. On this occasion I had a companion with me, so that we could keep the yacht sailing all the time to her best capacity, but allowing for this, it is a very high average and probably a record for a ship of her size. The run home from the Azores was spoilt by nearly a week of calm, so that the average fell to seventy-two miles a day.

Does one actually enjoy these long voyages? Rather a difficult question to answer. Definitely I would not undertake a long passage for its sake alone, but as the only possible means of reaching a new and desirable cruising ground they are well worth while. To my mind the greatest joy in yachting is to cruise along some lovely coast, finding one's way into all sorts of out-of-the-way coves and rivers. A pleasant day's sail of four to six hours, and then, perhaps, a beat up some narrow, winding river. Handling one's ship in narrow waters, preferably where one has never been before, is the finest sport in the world, which incidentally would be mostly gone if one had an engine; then a run ashore followed by a quiet evening in the cockpit watching the lights change over the calm water.

On the whole I enjoyed the voyage to Newfoundland. Mostly, the weather was favourable. As was to be expected in the summer, no desperate gales were encountered, and on most days good progress was made. I had no anxiety lest I should be unable to find my destination. The first gale during which the yacht was pooped rather frightened me; otherwise I kept in good spirits and never wished I had not started. The thrill of sighting America—I suppose one counts Newfoundland as America—was worth a dozen times the amount of discomfort which I had suffered.

The passage from Newfoundland to Bermuda was altogether different. It remains in my mind as twenty-three days of uninterrupted misery. I would have run back to St. John's or Halifax, only I just did not dare to recross the belt of cold water so late in the year. As will be related farther on, it is possible that I should have abandoned the yacht had the opportunity occurred. I could have withstood the discomfort and danger with more serenity of mind if it had not seemed probable that I should be unable either to reach the vicinity of Bermuda or to find the island if I succeeded in getting near it. For some time after my arrival I felt that I never wanted to see the sea or ships again.

The voyage home was neither pleasant nor the reverse. A return naturally lacks the thrill and excitement of a start. During the first stage there was the great satisfaction at the magnificent days' runs that we were making. My companion made the work much easier and more pleasant, though at times it was actually more strain with two than with one. With the wind aft we felt we must keep the ship going all we could, and this entailed long periods at the helm with careful steering. A part of one's watch below would be occupied with cooking, navigation, or domestic chores. After two or three days of this we both felt the strain decidedly; then the wind would shift and give us a rest while the ship sailed herself. Alone one could not have attempted to steer for such prolonged periods. The mainsail would have been lowered and the yacht left to run by herself under headsails. There was an entire lack of adventure or incident, and the voyage proceeded in a routine almost as in a liner. Writing now, two months after my return, I feel it will be about next spring before I am ready for another voyage.

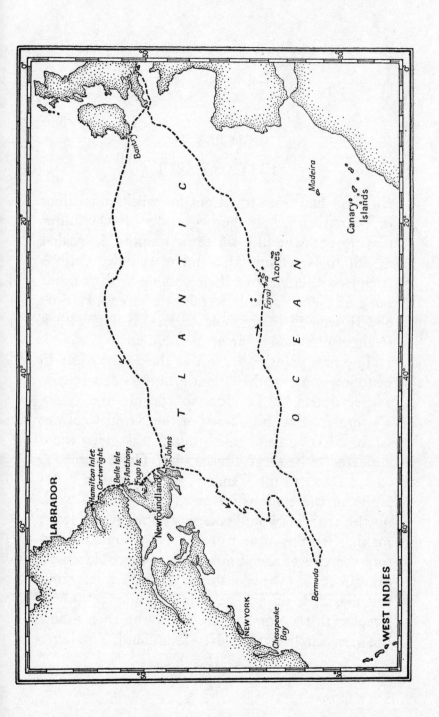

LABRADOR

Hamilton Inlet
Cartwright
Belle Isle
St.Anthony
Fogo Is.
St.Johns
Newfoundland

Banks

Madeira

Canary
Islands

Azores
Fayal

A T L A N T I C   O C E A N

NEW YORK
Chesapeake
Bay

Bermuda

WEST INDIES

CHAPTER III

THE START

EMANUEL had been fitted out for week-end sailing in March 1934. At the beginning of May, after playing with the idea for some months, I decided to sail to Newfoundland. I had sounded various friends with a view to their coming with me, but none of them was able to take the necessary time off. It seemed inadvisable to risk sailing with a stranger obtained by an advertisement.

The first point to settle was the actual route to be followed across the Atlantic, and for this I made a special trip to London to consult the *Ocean Passage Book* at the library of the Royal Cruising Club. Although not much detail was given there appeared to be three alternatives. These were: (1) to sail south to the Canary Islands, cross the Atlantic in the trade-wind belt, and then to work northward: this would take several months at least, making it impossible to reach Newfoundland before the end of the summer; (2) one could try to sail direct; or (3) make to the northward, crossing the meridian of 30° west in latitude 55° north (level with the north of Ireland), and then follow the great circle track to Newfoundland. The latter

32

gave the greatest probability of favourable winds, and I decided to adopt it. From a study of the Pilot Chart it was probable that for half the time the wind would be sufficiently to the north or to the south to make it possible to sail the course; for one-quarter of the time the wind would be directly ahead, and for the remainder there would be variable light airs or calms. On the average on one day in twenty it would blow a gale of force eight [1] or more.

In actual practice, I met more than my share of easterly or south-easterly winds. I estimated that the voyage would take thirty days, and decided to carry full provisions, including luxuries, for that period, with a reserve of biscuit and bully beef for another thirty days.

The question of food needed very careful thought. 'Ships are all right, it's the men in them,' says one of Conrad's characters. In yachts it is usually the crew which give out before the ship. Exhaustion and loss of morale are a direct consequence of lack of food. Moreover, especially by oneself, meals must be reasonably appetising. I made out a daily menu to be repeated each week. Breakfast would consist of some combination of eggs, bacon, fried tomatoes, or sardines. Dinner would be a light meal of bully beef, hard-boiled

[1] An arbitrary scale of numbers is used by seamen for recording the force of the wind.

eggs, tinned lobster or salmon. The afternoon would be broken by tea and toast, and for supper there would be some tinned meat ration or stew, ham or salt beef with tinned peas or beans, followed by fruit or asparagus and with raisins and nuts for dessert. Fresh bread and meat should last ten to fourteen days. The latter can be made into a stew, and will keep indefinitely if heated up each day.

When the bread was finished I should use sea biscuits. The modern type called cabin biscuit is very palatable, so that I gave up attempts to cook dough in the deep fry. Tinned soups are very useful as an emergency ration in bad weather or at night. I do not care much for alcohol, except for a bottle of beer with supper. I carry a bottle or two of rum or brandy, and take an occasional glass of neat spirit when cold or frightened. One bottle lasted for the whole of my first passage. At night coffee makes the best stimulant for those hours of the early morning between one and three when it may be necessary to stave off the craving for sleep.

Water is easily arranged for. *Emanuel*, not being built for ocean cruising, has only a small tank holding fourteen gallons. This is ordinarily augmented by two 'gem' tins holding another five and a half gallons. As a reserve three drums holding five gallons each were stowed beneath the cockpit. I knew from previous experience that without rationing oneself, but by exercising reasonable care, one would use half a gallon a day. One could probably manage on considerably less. Salt water can be used for washing, and for boiling potatoes or eggs.

The yacht herself needed little preparation. A new flax mainsail[1] had previously been ordered, and as I had not the heart to throw the old one away, it was retained on board as a spare, though I rather grudged the stowage space required for it. I carried a trysail, three jibs, two staysails, topsail, spinnaker, and dinghy's lugsail. The headsails were old, but in fair condition. As *Emanuel* would be manageable under any one of them it seemed safe to assume that all five would not be likely to be blown away. At a pinch the topsail, which by some curious error had been made of the same heavy canvas as the mainsail, could be set forward. Sufficient spare rope to renew all the running rigging was carried.

At last all was ready. The previous day I had said good-bye to my daughter, who had been my constant sailing companion for eleven years. It seemed a particularly treacherous proceeding sailing off without her, but she has her work. I am afraid she found it very hard to forgive me, though her last words were, 'Oh, well, fair winds, Daddy.'

Half an hour after noon on 11th May I hoisted

[1] The main boom is fitted with roller-reefing gear.

sail and slipped from my mooring at Lake, just above Poole. Mr. Knight, the foreman of the yard, knew where I was bound, but no one else. I did not know whether I was man enough to bring it off, and thought the less said the better. There was a light south-east air, and I tacked slowly down the harbour past the anchored yachts feeling very full of suppressed excitement. In light winds *Emanuel* is very easily handled by one person, and it was a very pleasant sail as far as the narrows off Sandbanks. Here the wind dropped almost to a calm, but the swift-running ebb carried the yacht seaward. Due to the tide there was a small but steeply vicious swell, so that it was necessary to work the sweep to keep the ship heading in the right direction. In the offing the tide would soon be running against me to the eastward, so, after passing the Bar buoy, I worked into Studland Bay and dropped anchor to await a more favourable wind. It seemed rather an ignominious start, and it would take a long time to reach Newfoundland at this rate. Still, I was quite glad of an afternoon's rest. I sleep in the afternoon whenever possible, so as to be prepared for the following night in case one has to keep awake all the time.

About 8 P.M. a very light south-east air was noticeable, so I set all sail, including topsail, and got up the anchor. Progress was very slow, and midnight found the yacht drifting becalmed half a mile south of Anvil Point lighthouse. By 3 A.M. I was feeling cold and drowsy. Supper (or breakfast) of eggs and bacon revived my spirits, and soon, with the growing light, I felt wide awake. A light northerly wind had made, and at 5 A.M. *Emanuel* was off the Shambles light-vessel, travelling well with the balloon staysail set. An hour later Portland Bill drew close. The tide was against me, though close inshore the water was fairly slack. Unfortunately under the cliffs there was no wind, so that I could not get round the Bill. It was very tantalising, since, a mile offshore, the waves were ruffled by a good breeze. After several attempts had failed I altered my course and stood out to sea. Noon found *Emanuel* completely becalmed five miles south of Portland. I took the opportunity to fit clip-hooks with an elastic band to the staysail halyards. This tip is from one of Conor O Brien's books, and saves time and trouble when shifting headsails. The patent log had been running very irregularly, so I took it to pieces, when it was apparent that the ball-race needed renewal. I tried to repair it and got it working again, but it was obviously under-logging and unreliable.

After lunch I had a couple of hours' sleep. Later in the afternoon there were variable airs which continued with intervals of calm throughout the night. I was well in the line of steamers proceeding up or down Channel, so had to keep awake, as there were generally five or six in sight. By 1 A.M. next morning the Bill was just dipping below the horizon. The breeze soon freshened, so that the topsail and balloon staysail had to come down. At 7 A.M. Start Point was abeam, and I realised that I had made a fast passage across West Bay.

After two nights out I felt that a good night's rest was needed, and directed my course towards Salcombe. I was unable to beat in over the tide, and had to anchor outside until 3 P.M. Then, with the flood, I sailed into the harbour. The wind, blowing from the cliffs, was very baffling, but with a clean bottom *Emanuel* handles easily to the slightest puff. The northern shore was quite blue from patches of flowers. After anchoring I went ashore for a stroll, and was surprised to see arum lilies flowering in the open as in South Africa.

During the passage I had tried out the new semi-rotary pump which had been installed in the cabin. It has a flexible rubber suction which is thrust through a hole in the floor-boards. There are two holes, so that by pumping from the lee one it is possible to free the ship and keep the bilge water off the cabin floor. The original pump, situated aft, will not free the ship when heeled, so that when beating to windward in a fresh breeze it was usual to have water showing on the lee side of the floor, which is bad for the morale as well as being uncomfortable. The new pump seemed very satisfactory. I spent quite a lot of time at it during a later portion of the cruise.

Next morning, on weighing the anchor, *Emanuel* seemed unduly sluggish. This was accounted for by a huge mass of seaweed which had wrapped itself round the anchor buoy. I stood out on the starboard tack, and found that I could steer about two points southward of the course for Falmouth. I spent most of the day searching for a leak. When punching into a head sea *Emanuel* has always made a little water; nothing serious, but enough to need a few minutes' pumping every hour or two. I took up the bottom-boards and shifted the ballast, but could find no sign of where the water came in. It was a dirty, tiring job, and at one time I felt squeamish. The cabin with table unshipped, floor-boards all awry, and with rusty iron bars piled in odd corners looked very depressing. The ship was sailing close-hauled, just carrying comfortably all plain sail. By 3 P.M. all was cleared up below, and I tacked, heading for Plymouth, where I intended to anchor for the night. An hour later the Eddystone was close abeam.

The 6 P.M. weather report spoke of the wind backing to south-west. This would entail a beat to Falmouth, whereas now, a mile off Rame Head, I could just lay the course. Accordingly I put about and stood on through the night. Although bitterly cold it was pleasant enough sailing along through the smooth sea. Daylight found *Emanuel* off St. Anthony Lighthouse at the entrance to Falmouth. With a dying breeze there was little chance of sailing over the foul tide, so I anchored outside. At mid-day I sailed in, anchoring among the other yachts at the far end of the harbour.

The next three days were occupied in embarking stores and writing farewell letters. I purchased an oil bag and a supply of oil for pouring on the water during storms, and replaced the defective parts of the patent log. My stores included ten pounds of salt beef, a portion pickled on shore, and the remainder put into brine; but I intended to put into some Irish port to fill up with water and fresh fruit at the latest possible moment. I tasted the reserve fresh water stored in old oil drums and found it quite sweet. It was a great business getting everything stowed away, but eventually a place was found for each article, and there was no outward sign, either in the cabin or on deck, that a long voyage was intended. A careful list was made of the contents of each locker.

On Saturday, 19th May, I awoke at 5.30 A.M. The weather report of the previous evening foretold easterly winds and fine weather. I weighed the kedge, hoisted the dinghy on deck, and made all preparations for sea. This is a lengthy job single-handed, and it was nine o'clock before I was able to get under way. Off St. Anthony the wind was

south-west, fresh, thus necessitating a beat out to
the Lizard, while at times rain obscured all visibility. At 12.45 P.M., when I sighted land half a
mile to the north, I was not sure whether it was
Black Head or the Lizard. It should have been the
former, but I had not kept a very accurate reckoning, and the apparent absence of any land beyond
for a few minutes gave rise to the hope that I had
weathered the Lizard. This was not the case,
however, as was soon obvious when the weather
cleared a few minutes later. This headland was
rounded about 4 P.M., after which there was rather
a tedious beat across Mounts Bay. The wind varied
from fresh to almost calm, but a considerable swell
persisted. I kept inside the stream of steamer
traffic, but there were a number of Brixham trawlers about, necessitating a careful look-out. At
midnight the Wolf Light showed up, and, the
wind backing a little, I was able to sail the course.
The Runnelstone buoy was passed at 4 A.M., after
which it was possible to shelter in the cabin for a
couple of hours with an occasional peep round the
horizon for passing ships. At 6 A.M. I was on deck
looking for the Seven Stones Lightship in very
poor visibility. I was not very sure of the exact
course made good for the last few hours, and might
have been heading for the shoal. Some ships were
in sight to starboard, which made it probable that
my course was a safe one, but it would have been

a desperate fiasco to have been wrecked at this early period of the voyage. However, a few minutes later the lightship hove in sight. It was drizzling and very cold, and the ship was carrying rather much sail for comfort. It is bad for a sail to be reefed when quite new, but by now my new mainsail should be pretty well stretched, so I rolled up a couple of turns. Backing the staysail, I then went below for breakfast. I felt a bit squeamish, no doubt due to fatigue after a rather tiring night, but I forced myself to cook, and after a good meal of sausages and bacon felt all right.

At 7.45 A.M. the Seven Stones bore south-west, distant four miles. I let draw the staysail and trimmed the sheets to sail north-west on my course for Ireland. The wind gradually increased and the motion became very violent, but the ship was making good progress. Shortly before noon further reduction of sail was necessary. I hove to and shifted jibs. It was rather a tussle on the forecastle, as the jib furling line carried away. The sail went overboard, and was pulled back with some difficulty. The jib outhaul had stranded, so I cut out the weak part and knotted the end to the traveller. I then reefed the staysail. A good deal of water was coming over forward. This work on the forecastle took about an hour, after which I returned to the cabin again, tired, damp, and feeling rather seasick. On this occasion rum and hot soup effected a cure.

I remained hove-to in order to rest, but was unable to sleep.

At 3.30 P.M. I let draw. My rough log notes wind moderating, but as this was entered after a substantial tea of buttered toast it may only have been the moral effect of food. However, *Emanuel* was sailing very easily about six points off the wind. There was a big swell from the west, apparently not caused by the present wind, which raised a short sea at an angle to the swell.

When reading the patent log at 8 P.M. I was rather disappointed to find the ship had been making only a fraction over four knots instead of about five, as I had supposed, but I was under very easy canvas. The reefs were retained, however, for comfort, as I was still rather tired. Side-lights were shipped and the anchor-light lashed to the stern of the dinghy. After supper I lay in the cabin, warm at last, listening to Albert Sandler's orchestra. The ship was steering a little to windward of the course.

May 21st. The day began with the same thick weather, heavy sky, and an intermittent drizzle; wind W.S.W., fresh, and sea moderate to heavy. Was there no sun? I had dozed from time to time, but got little sound sleep, as it had been necessary to look round the horizon every now and then in case of meeting ships. At 6 A.M. the log showed an average speed of 4.4 knots during the night. Anything over four knots I regard as satisfactory; five knots is good, and six, very rarely obtained, very good. At 7.35 A.M. a big sea broke on the cabin top and a heavy splash fell below. I pulled aft the hatch to prevent another.

While lifting the kettle at breakfast I sustained a small burn on my wrist. I dressed it with olive oil and lint. A sore spot just where the cuffs of one's oilskin chafe is rather troublesome. I was still feeling squeamish at times, and decided to make the nearest Irish port for a night's rest. At noon the ship had made a good ninety-two miles during the previous twenty-four hours. An hour later I altered course to N.N.W. to make the land. For the next six hours I sat at the tiller keeping a vigilant lookout. Visibility was very poor; at times only about half a mile.

7.15 P.M. Very cold and difficult to keep warm. It was now getting dusk, and it seemed unsafe to continue towards the land. Accordingly, I put about and hove to heading out to sea. The wind had decreased and the sea was much smoother, so that it was very comfortable below. *Emanuel* has a very easy motion for her size, on account of the greater part of her ballast being inside and not on the keel. I placed the lights as before, cooked a substantial supper, and lay down to sleep. I felt no anxiety over leaving the ship to look after herself. As I have previously explained, any alteration in the wind would have awakened me at once. The danger of being run down was slight. It was unlikely that chance should bring a ship very close. My lights were good, and by the rule of the road it was the duty of any passing ship to give way to me. *Emanuel*, hove-to, was moving only very slowly through the water. If she had been run down her aggressor would not have been damaged, so that I need have no fear that other lives were endangered.

I was on deck next morning at 4 A.M., feeling very fit and completely rested after nearly six hours' unbroken sleep. A small trawler was at work a mile or two away, and gave me the sense of company. There was a moderate westerly wind with fair visibility deteriorating to thick at times. After laying down my dead-reckoning position on the chart I steered north to make the land, estimated to be twenty miles away. I shook out the reefs, as full sail could be carried in comfort.

There is always great excitement at making a landfall after some days at sea. There had been no opportunity for sights, so that I might be considerably out of my position. I peered out eagerly over the grey waste of water, and at 7.15 A.M. a dull outline showed up ahead through the mist. It was land and not very far off. This coast was not familiar to me, but from the chart I was soon able to identify Badger Island in the sound between

Cape Clear Island and the mainland. This put me eight miles west of the D.R., which was satisfactory enough after sailing for two days in thick weather. The nearest harbour was the place for me, and I bore up for Baltimore, which lay a few miles to lee-ward. The entrance, between moderately high cliffs, is easy, and at 8.45 A.M. I anchored off the village. It is a magnificent natural harbour over a mile in extent and completely land-locked, though too shallow for big ships. The scenery is wild and desolate, the only buildings being the small village of Baltimore on the eastern shore. I went ashore for a walk and to post letters. Subsequently, I learned that when my wife saw the Baltimore postmark her first thought was that I had made a very quick passage to America. As only $5\frac{1}{2}d$. remained in the cash drawer I was not able to buy much, but it sufficed for my wants—*i.e.*, a $2d$. stamp and a jug of milk.

Later in the evening I sailed through the north-ern entrance to the harbour and looked at the alternative way out. I noted a mark for clearing Mealbeg rock, but any description would only be misleading without the chart. I anchored in the Sound near Black Rock in very lovely surround-ings. Rocky islands, some splashed pink with sea-thrift, lay all round. Neither boat nor house could be seen anywhere, and I seemed alone in the world. But not lonely; one only feels that in a town. An island close to the eastward was called Spanish Island on the chart. Perhaps some stragglers from the Armada landed there and were probably knocked on the head by the local inhabitants.

Next morning I weighed early to catch the tide and beat out northward through the Sound. It is a narrow, intricate channel encumbered by shoals and rocky islets, but with the large-scale Admiralty chart was not really difficult. In Long Island Bay the wind dropped entirely, and to prevent the yacht drifting back I dropped anchor off the Middle Calf Island. By the time I had finished breakfast there was again a light westerly wind, and all day I tacked backwards and forwards along the shore. It was a bright sunny day and very pleasant sailing along a coast which I had never seen before. I rounded Mizzen Head at 4 P.M., when the breeze degenerated into calms and light variable airs. As I approached Bantry Bay it got dark, and for some hours I lay without steerage-way. Presently there was a draught from the north, and I worked over towards Bere Island and through the west entrance into Berehaven, anchoring at 11 P.M.

May 24th. It was flat calm until 11 A.M., when I set sail to a cat's-paw from the south-west. Passing eastwards through Berehaven I could see the soldiers and the guns on the island. Not many people remember that this is one of the two places in the Free State where a British garrison is still

retained. A destroyer, H.M.S. *Versatile*, was anchored in the Haven, and I dipped my flag to her
as I sailed past. Off Roancarig at 12.50 P.M. there
was a slightly better breeze, to which I set the topsail and spinnaker, steering east for Bantry. It was
glorious sitting in the cockpit in the warm sun.
With a line round the tiller the ship slipped quietly
along, only now and then needing an extra touch
of the helm. I brought up an old pair of trousers to
darn and turned on the wireless.

I sailed into Bantry by the western entrance and
anchored close to a yacht called the *Waterwitch*.
Her owner, Mr. Patrick O'Keefe, made himself
known to me, and endeared himself by telling me
that he had bought a copy of my daughter's book
about our Faeroe Island cruise. He promised assistance with stores in the morning and took me up
to his house for supper, when I was introduced
to his charming wife. He told me some blood-
curdling tales of the time of the troubles.

Next morning I had breakfast with the O'Keefes,
who then took me round the town and helped me
lay in a stock of fresh provisions. We then went
for a motor run to Killarney, where we had lunch
at an hotel kept by relatives of O'Keefe. We
stopped on the way at Roches Hotel, Glengariff.
Most naval officers of the older generation know
that bar with its collection of nautical trophies.
The news that I intended sailing for America

had spread, and I was asked for my autograph! Mr. O'Keefe is the chief merchant of the town, and was most generous. His presents included a bottle of whisky, a pocket compass, a panama hat, oilcan, battery charging, vegetables, &c. But more than all this he took my trip to America as a matter of course and foretold a light-weather passage. This encouragement was indeed appreciated.

CHAPTER IV

CROSSING THE ATLANTIC

THE morning of 26th May broke fine and clear
with a light northerly wind, and conditions for a
start were propitious. I was awake early, making
preparations for sea, but now that the long-
awaited moment was at hand I felt curiously little
excitement. The dinghy was hoisted on deck by
the throat halyards and securely lashed; then, as
I was about to get up the mainsail, O'Keefe and
his man Mike came off to help. The latter hauled
up the anchor and O'Keefe took the helm for a few
minutes to see how *Emanuel* handled; then, with
last words of encouragement and a last grip of
the hand, they got into their dinghy and shoved
off.

I cruised around for a few minutes to give them
an opportunity to photograph *Emanuel*, and then
steadied on my course for the mouth of the bay.
As their figures faded into the distance and their
waving hands became indiscernible I felt a twinge
of loneliness, thinking that this was likely to be
my last human contact for many days.

With spinnaker and topsail set *Emanuel* glided
through the smooth water of Bantry Bay, and with

the sun shining brightly on the rugged hills all around me, it was easy enough to feel bold. The wind, however, gradually died away, and off Berehaven the yacht lay becalmed for some hours, while through my glasses I watched the soldiers on Bere Island. A steam drifter passed me flying the Spanish ensign. As she drew close I read the name *Porras* of Gijon, and wondered if she had been in that port when *Emanuel* visited the north coast of Spain some years ago. It was tiresome being delayed at the start by lack of wind, but my friends at Bantry were well out of sight and I was spared that awkward embarrassment of a prolonged farewell.

There is usually plenty to be done aboard a sailing ship. There was a small tear in the spinnaker that needed sewing, and then I dressed the main-sheet with olive oil. This made a dreadful mess on the counter, but the rope will now remain supple. It is a piece of four-stranded yacht manilla and becomes unpleasantly harsh when wet. Conor O Brien suggests that all ropes would be better if oiled occasionally, but more particularly I wanted to get rid of a can of olive oil which we had brought back from Spain and which had been lying about in the yacht ever since.

During the afternoon the wind gradually sprang up again, and *Emanuel* stood out to open sea close-hauled on the starboard tack. As she

drew clear from the shelter of the land a slight
chop rather checked her way and she became somewhat lively. I took in the topsail and big staysail so
that the motion should be more comfortable. As I
think I have already mentioned, it is the human
element that is the weakest link of the chain, and I
had decided that I must take things very easily and
on no account over-exert or tire myself out. Whenever the motion should be uncomfortable I would
shorten sail or, if I felt bored with steering when
she would not hold the course, I would heave to
or lower the sails. I would eat whatever and whenever I felt like it, and, in fact, would never allow
any effort of self-control to strain my nerves;
almost, one might say, I determined to live a life
of complete self-indulgence. I found this philoso-
phy entirely successful, but, when endeavouring
to prolong it to a shore life, certain difficulties
arise!

With the wind on the bow *Emanuel* sailed herself, and resting in the cabin I felt very secure and
comfortable. At 7 P.M. the land was fading into
the distance, and I took bearings of Mizzen Head
and Bull Point to fix my departure. The wind was
freshening somewhat, and an hour later my rule
of self-indulgence had to be put aside while I
dressed myself in oilskins and clambered forward
to the spray-swept forecastle to reduce sail. For a
couple of hours I wrestled with wet ropes and sod-

den canvas while I shifted jibs, reefed the staysail, and put a couple of rolls in the mainsail. I placed the navigation lights for the last time. In mid-ocean, off the steamer lanes, the chance of being run down was so utterly remote that it was not worth while carrying them.

The motion was now fairly violent, but I was able to heat up the remains of a stew and make a good supper. The glass was high, and the northerly wind presaged fine weather. The cabin, lit by a swinging lamp, seemed very cosy as I lay listening to all the little noises of the ship. The scrunch and splash of the water on the bows, the hum of the wind in the rigging, and the creak of the blocks made a pleasant chorus. I was so used to it that, instead of finding these noises discordant, they lulled me to sleep; nor did the motion keep me awake. Lying on the lee bunk, with my back against a cushion, I was securely wedged in place so that my body did not move as the ship lifted and curtsied to the waves. Up, down, lurch and splash, repeated with utmost regularity, told me that the ship was keeping to her course, while the same stars wheeled continually across the dark opening of the cabin hatch.

I woke at 2 A.M., and without going on deck glanced at the dimly lit compass under the bridge deck. She still holds her course north-west by west. Standing at the foot of the cabin stairs I glance round the horizon to find no lights in sight, and then curl up once more on my bunk.

I turned out at 5.30 A.M. One cannot afford to undress at night, so that getting up entails nothing but a shake of the body and a sponge over one's face. Sleeping in one's clothes entails no discomfort whatsoever after a little practice. There was, of course, now no land in sight. Wind and sea had gone down very much, and the dancing, bright-blue waves seemed friendly. Under the sun lay a dazzling golden path leading from the yacht to the horizon. A small trawler was at work a mile away, and nearly ahead was a white-painted steamer apparently stopped in the water. The latter seemed rather mysterious, but I did not pass near enough to read her name. In these days of peace there must have been some innocent justification for her presence; probably she was repairing a telegraph cable.

I let out the reefs and then breakfasted in great comfort on eggs and bacon. After this I had sufficient energy to hoist the topsail and big staysail. The ship continued to hold her course, ghosting along at about two knots, while, as usual, I found plenty of odd jobs to do. There was a tiny chafe in the working staysail that needed a stitch; the fall of the runner purchase was chafing against the dinghy, and some old canvas had to be tied round it to prevent the rope cutting through the planks;

then the anchor was unstocked and put below and the navel pipe plugged with a cork. It is not often that the cable is unbent in a yacht, and I thought of the descriptions one reads about the old square-riggers putting to sea and in which this is the usual routine.

The day passed very pleasantly; the run (always counted from noon to noon) was eighty-four miles, which was fairly satisfactory, though when I pricked off the position on the chart it seemed a very tiny portion of the blank expanse before me. I was not impatient, however. Some 1,700 miles of ocean lay ahead, and reaching port was so utterly remote that I did not think of it. My life was the present—living and sailing in my comfortable little ship for an indefinite period. The wireless was very companionable, and I enjoyed the music, but, cut off as I was from the rest of the world, the news was of indifferent interest, while I should soon be outside the area covered by the British weather reports. In any case, these latter were of little interest. I should know very well if there was a gale approaching and there is always ample time to reduce sail without any outside warning. In fact, it is better not to know too far ahead. I am much too far out to have any thought of running back for shelter, and must take the weather as I find it. *Emanuel* has never encountered a full gale in the open sea, but I am pretty confident that she will ride out in safety whatever may come, and it will be interesting to put my theoretical knowledge to the test; but the start of the voyage is suspiciously easy.

After supper the wind freshened a little, so that I got down the topsail and big staysail; but in any case I should not like to turn in with all the kites set. The oil from the main-sheet was still making a horrible mess on the counter.

During the night the wind almost died away; some adjustment of sheets and helm was necessary at midnight, but at 4 A.M. it was practically calm. From midnight to noon the yacht only sailed sixteen miles, and during the afternoon there was not even steerage way; but the bright sun made the day very pleasant, and a gentle swell caused only a slight roll.

At lunch I drew water from the tank for the first time; till then the full kettle and saucepan had sufficed. I had a large reserve, and was likely to use only half the actual supply. A tramp steamer passed during the afternoon, but she was a long way off and probably never noticed *Emanuel*.

My rough log contains notes as to the consumption of stores, of no general interest, but useful to myself so that I should know if any economy might be needed.

The calm continued all night till 6 A.M. next morning (29th May), when a light easterly air sprang up. I set the topsail and spinnaker, and all day the yacht ran gently before the wind, making between two and three knots. Sometimes I would sit at the tiller and steer, but when I needed food or was otherwise occupied I found that the helm could be lashed; she would then hold the course for a few minutes or perhaps for half an hour at a time, after which she would wander off one way or the other and get one of the sails aback unless I noticed and was able to jump to the tiller in time. I must have been up and down the cabin stairs some hundreds of times.

During the morning a small bird alighted on the ship. It was about the size of a sparrow, with a blunt beak, red face, white breast, conspicuous blue back, black wings, and a fine forked tail. It seemed a friendly little thing, perching on the tiller and then on my finger. I provided water, bread crumbs, &c., but it would take nothing. After an hour's rest it seemed to cheer up and began to chirp; then it went below and explored the cabin, after which it flew away. I hope my friendly little visitor reached land, but it was a long way for such a tiny bird. I can only suppose that it had been carried north-ward from the West Indies on board a fruit steamer.

The wind continued steady all day. It seemed a pity to waste it, so I remained at the helm, carrying topsail and spinnaker after the sun had set. There is an extension wire for the headphones so that I can wear these when steering, and I found it very pleasant listening to the dance music as hour succeeded hour. At 1.30 A.M. the wind had veered to the south, so that the spinnaker would no longer draw and had to come in. Then, taking in the top-sail, the ship would look after herself while I snatched a few hours' rest.

Next day passed without much incident; still steering to the north-west with the wind about abeam. During the afternoon I heard a groaning aloft and clambered up the mast to investigate. The parrel wire of the gaff had broken, and a knot in the wire had chafed the mast rather badly. I removed the wire and smeared tallow in the jaws. I cannot imagine how the wire, which was new, had broken. There is no difficulty in going aloft in moderate weather when sail is set to steady the ship.

May 31st. Was not so pleasant. I was wakened at 5 A.M. by the flapping of the sails, and found it drizzling, with a fresh north wind. I reefed down, feeling rather gloomy, as one's vitality is at a low ebb at this hour. It looked a proper dirty morning, but the glass showed nothing. Breakfast was taken under some difficulty owing to the violent motion. I started a side of bacon, but forgot to wash the salt off it; the rashers were just eatable. After breakfast I was more able to appreciate the fact that *Emanuel* was making excellent progress, but with the wind on the bow she was bucking into the sea and was very skittish. I felt the motion somewhat and spent a slack morning in the cabin with a book. The wind went light in the afternoon, and I lowered the mainsail to fit a new parrel. There was a big north-westerly swell and not enough wind to steady the sails, so that the slatting of the gear became unpleasant.

At 6.45 P.M. a large freighter was observed approaching on the bow. I put up a red ensign and she did the same. As she came close I read the name *Fishpool* of West Hartlepool. I could see her crew lining the deck and gazing down on the little craft alongside. I had no signal flags on board, and was particularly anxious not to give rise to the impression that I needed help, or to delay her in any way. With their glasses they would be able to see every movement, so I went below very deliberately, fetched a tin of cigarettes, and opened it. I gave one wave of the arm to which all her crew replied with similar gestures, and then she passed on. As she drew away her ensign fluttered half-way down the staff, and I lowered mine in reply. This silent courtesy of the sea gave me as great a sense of companionship as any spoken word could have done.

Later all the sails were lowered to avoid the chafing of the gear as the calm continued and the yacht rolled heavily. I spent quite a long time tracking rattles in the cabin. After supper I remember sitting for a while in the cockpit watching the increasing swell. In the half-light the gently rounded waves looked dark and sleek, and each one rolled up astern with sinister and menacing aspect.

The night remained calm, but a southerly air sprang up in the early morning. I made sail at once, setting the spinnaker from the end of the bowsprit, but by 8 A.M. the wind had veered a little and was increasing. The strain of the spinnaker halyards was pulling the top of the mast forward and bending it about rather like a fishing-rod (*Emanuel* has no topmast backstay), so this sail had to come in, the big staysail being set in its place. At 10 A.M. my log notes 'Ideal conditions, wind fresher, making five knots in glorious sunshine. This is what one pictures to oneself when planning a voyage; morale very high at the moment.'

I sowed mustard and cress on a damp flannel, but for some reason the growth was poor, possibly not enough light in the cabin.

During the afternoon the wind increased, and for some hours *Emanuel* was making six knots, but with the stronger wind the sea got up and the yacht began to pound into the waves. As her bow met each crest the water broke over the forecastle in a seething mass of white, and then, flooding aft to the break of the cabin, rose in a cloud of spray which drove back over the cockpit.

Towards evening the motion became very violent, and I suffered from a minor attack of nerves, recalling all the tales of disaster that I had ever read, any of which might happen to my ship. It was quite unreasonable; one might as well drive a motor-car wondering all the time if a wheel was coming off or if the steering gear was about to jam. Probably I had been smoking and sitting still in the cabin too much. However, it was time to shorten sail. The big staysail was a nasty sodden mass of canvas, but it stowed very conveniently in the dinghy. The latter makes a very useful receptacle for odds and ends when at sea. Many thanks, too, to O Brien for his tip of clip-hooks with an elastic band instead of the tiresome business of unshackling the halyards or mousing a hook. The working staysail has double sheets with bee-blocks shackled to the clew. When hoisting it in a fresh breeze these blocks flap from side to side with great violence unless someone is aft to steady in the sheet. It is rather a business climbing about from end to end of the ship a dozen times when dressed up in oilskins, sea-boots, and lifeline. Later I gave up wearing a lifeline, as it occurred to me that if I did fall overboard I should never be able to haul myself back.

Falling overboard is perhaps the chief danger in a yacht. One could not very well fall out of the cockpit, and when working forward the danger is so very immediate that one automatically guards against it by continually holding on to some rope. In bad weather it is quite impossible to stand without support, and most of the work is done on one's hands and knees. In a big ship, where huge masses of solid water may break on board, it is not uncommon for a man to be torn from his hand-hold and washed overboard. *Emanuel* is so buoyant that I do not think this could happen aboard her.

The action of shortening sail dispelled the attack of nerves, and I went below to make a curry for supper. I can only conveniently use one saucepan, so the rice, steak, raisins, and curry powder are all put in together.

I did not like pounding into the sea so heavily while I slept, so hove to under very reduced sail. With her way thus checked, it was very comfortable in the cabin, gently rising and falling to the waves.

Next morning broke with a dull, gloomy, overcast sky, but the sea had gone down somewhat and I was soon sailing fast with the wind abeam. A good deal of spray drove over the ship, but she had made very little water during the night. I had tacked a piece of oiled calico over the hinges of the cabin skylight, which stopped the drip that had occasionally been noticeable before. My bread had developed a thick coating of mould, but the inner portion of the loaf was quite sweet.

The day's run was 112 miles, the best of the whole voyage, though when I pricked off the position it was obvious that the ship was considerably to the southward of the proposed track. I had been a week at sea, and was very well satisfied with the progress made.

I had bad luck at lunch. Opening a tin of supposed tongue I found date jam, which had been purchased in Spain some years previously. It was quite sweet, but I do not care for any jam. There were a number of old tins on board which I wanted to use up before starting the new supply; but I had ample food for several months. The tinned stews, of which I had allowed one per meal, contained enough for two or three meals, and the fresh provisions were lasting far longer than I had estimated. My new supplies were in lockers that do not usually get wet, and should retain their labels.

During the afternoon the sea was smoother, and I was able to have a really good wash and change of linen. The salt-water soap was reasonably satisfactory. After that I was busy with needlework, as my clothes were showing signs of wear. For my next voyage I should like a complete trousseau, or else to ship a female crew who could sew flags, clothes, and sails; but perhaps my wife would object to that.

Towards sunset the wind freshened, and *Emanuel* had to be close reefed. I remember standing at the foot of the cabin stairs watching the yacht glide into great valleys of water and then climb slowly up the next slope. These ocean rollers are so long from crest to crest that the ship has plenty of time to adjust her position easily to the slope of the water without that jerky motion occasioned by a short sea. I rested below throughout the night, but did not sleep much.

At 2.30 A.M. the chain plate of the weather backstay was found to be broken. This is not so serious as it sounds. Mr. Anderson, *Emanuel*'s builder, once said that he only fitted backstays to give a hand-hold when going forward. An alteration in the lead of the backstay put matters right, after which I hove-to to get a better rest. At daylight, after rolling up a little more of the mainsail, I let draw.

For breakfast I poached a couple of eggs, using salt water. The result was not satisfactory, but I managed to eat them. Later I found myself with a headache, most unusual when yachting, and took a dose of calomel. The sea continued to increase, and heavy splashes swept across the cockpit. One struck my back with a thud and then cascaded down the cabin stairs. Thanks to an efficient oilskin only my arms got wet. There was too much spray and motion for sights, but the log at noon registered another 109 miles. I was, however, getting too far to the south and close to the steamer track, which I particularly wished to avoid. The wind being southerly, *Emanuel* would not hold a course northward of west without being steered, and, anyway, was now rather pressed even with her close-reefed mainsail. It seemed time to get this down; I pulled the sheet right in, set up the topping lift, and let go the throat halyards. Then, when the peak halyards had been eased a little, I was able to gather in the leach of the sail and lash it to the boom. The yacht rolled horribly, and I lashed the boom to the gunwale to prevent it swinging from side to side. There remained only a small part of the sail with the gaff sagging out to leeward. I lowered the peak halyards again, and was able to pull in the rest of the sail. This getting the mainsail down in a gale of wind is a lengthy business, as there is so much crawling from end to end of the ship; but with more practice I got expert at it.

I had never had occasion to run before the wind under headsails, and was anxious to see how the ship would behave. With the helm lashed amidships she steered herself pretty well to the north-west with the wind on the port quarter, though at times yawing wildly so that the sea was brought nearly abeam. For the next six hours she averaged five knots. It was astonishingly quiet and comfortable in the cabin in spite of an occasional heavy roll. My headache had gone, but it was unfortunate that a dose of calomel had been necessary at the commencement of bad weather. The barometer had been falling all day, though the weather remained fine and sunny. The cabin doors had been shipped to keep out the spray; no heavy water came over the stern, and the yacht seemed running very safely.

After supper I lay down to rest; at 1 A.M. a terrific crash woke me. I jumped up from my bunk to see water streaming solidly down through the louvres of the cabin doors, and it flashed through my mind that the ship was sinking. I pushed open the doors and saw the cockpit full of water, but as I became fully awake I realised that the ship was sailing on and apparently unharmed. It was too dark to see what the sea was like, but the white breaking crests of the waves could be made out all around. The air was so full of driven spray that the drizzling rain was hardly noticeable. Being pooped like this was a new experience altogether, and I did not want it to be repeated. From the books I had read I knew exactly what to do, and had, in fact, thought it out beforehand. A big hawser was got out from under the cabin bunk; some old coils of rope were secured to the end of it, which was then paid out over the stern. In the blackness of the night, and almost blinded by spray and rain, it was no easy matter wrestling with these heavy stiff coils of rope, and I had to be careful that the hawser did not take charge and pull me overboard. Then, crawling forward to the forecastle, I got down the jib. Sprawling on all fours and clutching desperately at the reeling deck, I let go the necessary ropes and dragged in the dripping sail. All the while the ship rolled and pitched, tossing her bows like a horse its head when tormented by flies. Badly I needed a third hand, but a rope's end can be held in one's teeth. Then aft again to get out another hawser from under the cockpit and to pay it out astern from the other side of the counter. The ship was now driving ahead under only a reefed staysail at two or three knots. The two hawsers astern checked her speed, so that instead of being carried forward with the waves she rose easily and allowed them to pass.

The above few lines represent some three hours' hard struggle. There was nothing more that could be done, so I returned to the cabin, boiled some soup, and changed into dry clothes. I then went to sleep.

When the day broke I could see through the driving rain how big the waves really were; it would have been bad weather for an Atlantic liner. As the ship rode to the top of each wave one looked out over mile after mile of grey watery ridges, each capped by a crest of foaming white. Now was the testing time of all our glib fireside talk on the management of yachts in bad weather. Tossed by the waves can have a very literal meaning; at times the yacht was flung bodily from summit to trough, but each time, just when it seems that an advancing wave must engulf the whole ship, she rises securely; she gives a wriggle and a toss, and then the wave passes harmlessly forward, while the yacht descends gently into the trough and points her stern to the next roller. Heavy splashes drove over the cockpit, when a breaking crest just happened to catch the stern, but no weight of water came on board. I stood for some time at the cabin hatch watching the seas, and complete confidence returned to me. From the way *Emanuel* rose to each wave, it seemed as if she must be possessed of a living cunning.

In spite of the heavy motion, a kettle was boiled and bacon fried. Tinned cream for the tea and a dessert of grape-fruit and nuts. My daughter will smile when I mention that the tea had a flavour of soup.

The falling curve of the barograph had now flattened out, and I judged that the centre of the disturbance was abreast of me. At 9 A.M. the wind was taking off and the rain was pouring down in large drops instead of driving in thin sheets. It had been a very clear case of 'wind before the rain.' A little later I was able to haul in the stern hawsers and make sail. At noon my longitude was 28° 34′

west, half-way to Newfoundland if I count the distance from Poole.

During the afternoon the wind fell completely, leaving the yacht to roll in a very high irregular swell. Steep pyramids of water seemed advancing from different directions, for all the world like a sea of moving sand-dunes. Every now and then a deep pit would seem to open suddenly, and the yacht would fall into it, reaching the bottom with a sharp jerk. The gear slatted from side to side, jarring the whole ship in spite of extra guys and lashings. The topsail sheet was used as a vang in an effort to steady the gaff, but after an hour or so the noise and the chafe became unbearable, and all sail was lowered. Poor *Emanuel* then rolled and pitched even more unmercifully.

There was plenty to do: stowing the hawsers away took some time; a couple of reef points on the staysail needed renewing, and the dinghy had to be replaced with the lashings tautened. The main shrouds had got rather slack; while setting up the bottle-screws a pair of pliers was lost overboard. Another pair was on board, so this did not matter. I noticed that the glass was rising very steeply, and found that the clockwork had stopped, thus accounting for the vertical rise. It started again with a shake.

The calm persisted all night, with the swell gradually going down. In spite of the motion I slept soundly for six hours. At 3 A.M. next morning (5th June) a light south-east air was noticeable; all sail was set, and *Emanuel* was soon running goose-winged before the breeze. In the confused swell that still persisted she would not steer herself at all well, and my breakfast of scrambled eggs was continually interrupted by the necessity to jump on deck and readjust the tiller. Scrambled eggs provide a convenient meal when there is much motion, as they can be eaten direct from the saucepan without the bother of a plate sliding from side to side of the table.

To avoid the bother of frequently going on deck, I fitted lines leading from the tiller to the cabin so that it was possible to steer from below. At first it was very confusing watching the afterside instead of the fore-side of the compass, and several gybes occurred before I automatically pulled the correct line.

For several days a number of stormy-petrels had been flying close to the ship. They are companionable little black-and-white birds, and continually fluttered just above the waves within a few yards of the stern. On this day some much larger white birds with very long tails were seen; they circled overhead, keeping at a good height.

The wind freshened during the day, and sail had to be gradually reduced. Towards evening the drizzling rain and falling glass showed that another gale was to be expected. As I lay resting in the cabin a smell of burning wool became noticeable; a new pair of serge trousers had been hung up to dry over the galley stove and had fallen on to the flames. Before they could be rescued large holes had been burned in each leg, and they were new, too.

By 9 P.M. the mainsail had to come down, and just before midnight the stern hawsers were got out again; but it was great good fortune that the wind continued from the south-east, and was blowing me ahead instead of backwards.

During the night the staysail gave trouble, flogging from side to side as the ship yawed wildly before the heavy seas. After listening to it for some time from the cabin I could bear the noise no longer. My supply of dry clothes was getting short, so before going on deck I changed into things that were already wet. Coming out of the cabin, the seas were rather scaring as each wave raged up astern. I rather funked going forward; the ship did not seem to be sailing too fast, but I was afraid the sail would blow away, and nerved myself to crawl forward and pull it down. This left the ship with only a storm jib of nine square feet set, so she was practically under bare poles. It was pleasant to get below again and to change into dry clothes, but it was impossible to sleep. The ship seemed to be making rather more water than

could be accounted for by the occasional splashes
over the cockpit; so far nothing serious, and three
or four minutes' pumping each hour freed the
ship. After the gale of two nights before I was not
worried about the sea, and I firmly believe that
Emanuel would ride through anything short of a
hurricane. It does not seem to matter which end
she points to the waves as long as she is not moving
too fast; but the way the ship is quite literally flung
from crest to trough must be a frightful strain on
the hull, and ships do spring leaks in bad weather—
lots of them—and while lying in the cabin I
remembered every story I had ever read of leaking
vessels and shipwrecked crews. There is, or used
to be, at one of the London galleries a picture by
Hemy of a ship in distress with the crew toiling
at the pumps. The ragged clothes of the men and
their exhausted features were vividly in my mind
as I knelt on the cabin floor and worked the pump
handle to and fro. As the ship rolled, the water
swished from side to side; but it was quite easily
kept under without any fatigue, and as long as the
ship held together I knew I was safe. Oh, Mr.
Anderson,[1] I hope there is no tiny detail of
scamped work nor any scrap of doubtful material
in *Emanuel* this night! But when this sort of idea
comes into one's head it is generally a sign that one
is needing a meal. My log continues: '3 A.M.

[1] *Emanuel's* builder.

Barometer starting to rise, hurrah. 6.15 A.M. Wind veering and moderating; set reefed staysail to help stop the rolling; with considerable effect; heading north; estimated run for the night N.N.W. 2½ knots, but it is, of course, only a guess. How delightful to have no land within 800 miles to worry about.

'8.40 A.M. Wind W.S.W., quieter; very little water made during the last two hours, so that's all right.

'9.45 A.M. Fresh breeze only, set close-reefed mainsail. It goes up bit by bit without much trouble.'

Crawling aft to the counter a few minutes later to read the log, I had not bothered to put on my oilskin, which was now showing signs of wear. I saw a big wave approaching, and made a dive, head first, through the cabin hatch, but not quite quickly enough, and a heavy splash fell on to my back. The wind gradually took off, and more sail was set as required. During the afternoon I patched the burned trousers, making an excellent job of it and one which I showed with great pride to several visitors later on. My clothes were getting rather short, as my other pair of working trousers had gone at the seat, and I did not want to spoil my shore-going kit. For supper the last of the steak stew was used up. It looked pretty nasty, but tasted very good; eleven days out.

Soon after dark the wind went very light, and in the confused swell the ship would not hold her course. After the previous broken night I felt that sleep was more important than a rather ineffectual effort to make progress. I lowered all sail and slept solidly for six hours.

Next morning was bright and sunny; after making sail and getting breakfast the cabin cushions were dragged up on deck to dry. For lunch I used the last of Mr. O'Keefe's lettuces. Standing in a mug of precious fresh water they had kept very well.

At noon I was exactly half-way between Bantry and St. John's. A tramp steamer was sighted three miles ahead, steering to the south-west. It gave me a great thrill to see another vessel, but she proceeded on her way without turning towards me. *Emanuel*, in a big swell, is a very small mark to pick up, and she probably never saw me.

It was a glorious yachting day, bright and sunny, and the sea was gradually getting smoother. Hour after hour the ship sailed on before the light easterly air, and for thirty-six hours she hardly needed any attention. I fitted new jib-sheets in place of the old ones, which were worn out. In the afternoon I measured the water-tank, and found that about six gallons had been used. This was the expected consumption of half a gallon per day. For supper I got out the pickled salt beef; it was a

74

grim story—part of the joint was alive with maggots. The other part looked all right, and, slicing it up, I put it on to stew. The smell was rather strong, but perhaps only normal, and it tasted quite good. An hour and a half later I felt the suspicion of a pain in the stomach, which I could not help connecting with the beef—probably wrongly, but anyway the rest of it went overboard. I suffered no more pains.

The spinnaker was showing a nasty tear in the foot. I did not like to risk it blowing away and perhaps fouling aloft during the dark hours, and replaced it by the big staysail, first cutting off the spring hooks after the advice of Mr. Gibbons of the *Ariel*. These hooks are liable to fasten themselves to the stays aloft when the sail is set on the spinnaker boom.

Emanuel continued to sail herself. It was a pity to waste the fair wind, and I decided to keep watch through the night. I had a fore guy on the main boom, and the spinnaker outhaul was taken forward. These would make a gybe less likely.

It was delightful sitting in the cockpit throughout the night while the ship glided steadily on, making five miles each hour. I wore the headphones, and, listening to the dance music from Fécamp, felt that there was no one in the world with whom I would willingly change places. Although there was no moon it was not really dark, and there was a reddish glow around the northern horizon nearly all night. I did not feel in the least lonely. Perhaps one's ship is company, and the low swish and gurgle of the water as she cuts through the waves is her voice speaking to me. During the previous gale I was glad to be alone without the responsibility of drowning someone else. I picked up very faintly some broadcast which seemed to come from America. The only audible words were 'New York,' but these excited me greatly. At 2.30 A.M. I had supper of coffee, sardines, and dessert.

The weather continued fine all through the next day, but with drifting patches of fog. Early in the morning the jaws of the gaff were found to be giving trouble again. I lowered the gaff, enlarged the jaws with a chisel, and then replaced the leather. For breakfast I had to use hard tack—ship's biscuit—as the last half-loaf of bread had gone mouldy all through. One of the Primus stoves needed constant pumping. On testing it in a bucket of water a small leak was discovered near the burner. It was still usable, and I could probably repair it with solder.

I was anxious to get a time signal, and to improve the aerial I connected a wire to the foretopmast stay. Lying out on the bowsprit to do this I got the lower part of my body wet, but in the bright sun the simplest way to dry one's clothes

76

was to wear them. One cannot catch cold from salt water. The Daventry time signal came through very faintly.

Just before noon the topsail had to come in, and with the freshening wind the yacht would no longer steer herself. I needed sleep. With drastic reduction of sail *Emanuel* was made to lie W.S.W. a couple of points to the southward of the course, and I went below after taking in the patent log. I suspected that the wind might go light, in which case the yacht would gybe, and probably the main-sheet would foul the bracket of the log. It has several times been damaged in this way.

Next day, 9th June, completed the second week at sea. During the last two days I had run 205 miles, and was now only 626 miles from St. John's. It was beginning to appear a manageable distance, and I was now looking forward to the end of the voyage, calculating on what day it might be possible to arrive. For a time I ran with the big staysail sheeted across the deck, tack hauled out half-way along the spinnaker boom. This seemed enough sail for her in a strong wind. I do not think a square-sail would be satisfactory when single-handed. My spinnaker boom would serve very well for a yard (by Worth's formula it is the right length), but it might be awkward to handle on that reeling forecastle, and whenever the wind freshened I should be wondering if it

77

were not time to get it down. The strong south-
easterly wind continued, and by noon on the
10th I had run another 101 miles. Nothing of
interest occurred until the evening of the next day.
I had been reaching out with the wireless and
listening to oscillations and unidentified whisper-
ings; then suddenly I heard, quite plainly, 'This
is the Dominion Broadcasting Company, St.
John's, Newfoundland.' Well, I must be sailing
something like the right direction, anyway. Later
a steamer's lights were seen passing; I called her
up with my torch, asking for information about
ice, but her reply was made too fast for me to read,
as I am not at all proficient at Morse.

June 12th found *Emanuel* running to the westward before a strong wind and heavy sea. I had
now reached the area in which ice might be encountered, and it was advisable to have some after-
canvas ready to set at a moment's notice. There
was too much wind for the whole mainsail, which
should have been partially rolled up before lower-
ing, and I considered bending the trysail. However, I attempted rolling up the mainsail first.
This is a very awkward job with the sail lowered
and the yacht rolling violently. If the main-sheet is
eased, the boom sweeps from side to side in a
devastating manner. I put various lashings round
boom and gaff, and hoisted the latter a shade.
After a two-hour struggle I got the sail more or

less rolled up, though it was impossible to get the turns evenly on the boom, and I feared that the sail would be stretched out of shape if it had to be hoisted in a gale. The wind moderated, and during the night backed to north-east. I continued all day sailing comfortably to the W.N.W., and it was very pleasant to see the governor wheel of the patent log spinning rapidly instead of merely idling.

The thought of icebergs was very much in my mind, as the Ocean Passage Book states that they may be encountered within 500 miles of Newfoundland. There was also the possibility of field ice, which really would be rather awkward for a ship like mine. I remembered the loss of the *Titanic* very well. At the same time I was very loath to waste any of a fair wind. The seas are wide, and if no ice were seen during the day the risk of actually running into a berg during the short hours of darkness was slight and could be accepted.

At 2.45 A.M. on the 14th I woke to find that the ship had gybed and had hove herself to on the other tack. The wind had gone light, but it was rather disturbing to find that I was sleeping so soundly that the actual gybe did not wake me. The weather was getting very cold, and my log notes that I was wearing three jerseys, two pairs of trousers, and extra stockings. I had evidently reached the cold Labrador current.

During the afternoon the St. John's broadcast came through in full loud-speaker strength. The advertisements were most interesting, and I felt that I was beginning to know this town with its Water Street, General Post Office, and shops which had just received a consignment of the latest Paris fashions.

Minor renewals, including a jib outhaul and a staysail tack lashing, were needed this day. So far nothing of importance has carried away, but the spinnaker gear is not heavy enough for prolonged use. Fog set in at dusk, and the wind died away, leaving the yacht to drift through the night; but at least I could sleep soundly without the fear of running into ice.

The calm continued till noon next day, and the run was only twenty-five miles; but I was glad to get sights, as there had been none for four days. My latitude was only six miles out, but it was disappointing to find by an afternoon sight that the ship was twenty-seven miles farther away from my port than had been reckoned. I had been unable to pick up any definite time signal, and the error of the watch was dependent on an announcement from St. John's that it was now three and a half minutes past two by the electric clock, Newfoundland daylight saving time. The Sailing Directions stated that the standard time of Newfoundland was 2 hours 31 minutes slow on Greenwich; presumably their summer time was one hour in advance, but it all seemed rather vague.

A fresh easterly breeze sprang up after lunch, and I felt glad to be sailing again. For supper a ham was boiled, which, with onions and potatoes, afforded a most palatable meal. It had been foggy for most of the day.

At midnight sail had to be shortened. The damp ropes were incredibly cold, and after a few minutes' work my fingers were numbed; but the sea was fairly smooth, so that it was dry in the cockpit.

I continued at the helm all night. Once a breaking crest showed white and gave me a start, thinking it was ice. The morning lightened imperceptibly, showing a dull, leaden sky and grim, grey seas. It was really very cold, and I piled on clothes, but was still unable to keep warm. I had no gloves, so pushed my hands into a pair of thick socks. Two stoves had been burning in the cabin throughout the night.

With the full daylight I fancied that there was a change in the formation of the waves difficult to describe, but perhaps the waves were smaller and steeper. The banks should have been fifty miles away, so that it was not likely to be due to shallower water. The mist continued; while drowsing at the helm a dirty white object caught my eye. It was just under the lee bow, but before the helm could be touched the yacht had sailed over it. My heart seemed to come up to my mouth. I stood up trembling, but could see nothing either ahead or astern, and there had been no jar nor grating of the keel. Then a porpoise provided the explanation as it showed its white-coloured belly.

June 17th was another day of calm and also of fog. Now that my port was not far off, the enforced delay and inaction were very irksome. For days I had seemed to be living in a little world of my own only about 500 yards across. During the morning my sense of isolation was suddenly broken by the sound of a steamer's syren. I jumped below to get my fog-horn, and replied with three short blasts, the signal for a ship running before the wind, though, in fact, the yacht had barely steerage way. It is not likely that the puny squeak of my instrument was heard on board the steamer. For a time the noise of her syren increased; then it gradually died away, and my world contracted to its original isolation. The steamer never came into view.

The damp fog was penetrating every corner of the ship, and even the blankets were getting damp. I rigged clothes lines across the cabin and kept a stove burning continually. Only about half the stock of paraffin had been expended, so that no economy was needed. During the afternoon there was sufficient wind to sail, and I kept watch till midnight. The ship was then hove-to so that I could rest, as it seemed wise that I should husband my strength. If field ice should be encountered, it might be necessary to sail the ship and to keep on the alert for a prolonged period.

After four hours below I was eager to be getting on. The wind continued fresh from E.N.E., with the weather still thick and bitterly cold. I was quite unable to bear sitting in the cockpit and steered from below, taking a look round the horizon every few minutes. Having seen no ice, I was beginning to think that the bergs were merely a figment of the unduly pessimistic Sailing Directions, though as a matter of fact I had seen ice in the Atlantic on previous voyages.

At 9.20 A.M. the fog lifted suddenly. Fine on the weather bow and four or five miles distant was a white shape. It gave me a great start, and I stood up, every muscle taut. So icebergs really do exist. As I approached it could be seen to consist of three pinnacles, two tapering up to thin, sharp spires, and the centre one truncated. It looked an enormous mass, but I hesitate to give an estimate in figures. The Sailing Directions recommend passing to windward to avoid small lumps of ice floating to leeward. Presently I went below to prepare my camera. Returning on deck I glanced ahead, but could see no berg. I had noted its bearing and looked at the compass for its exact direction. There, perhaps a half, or perhaps a quarter of a mile distant, was just perceptible for a few seconds a ghastly white shape, half of it draped as if by a sheet, the fog. The curtain drew across, hiding it entirely. Single-handed in mid-Atlantic is no occasion to go seeking icebergs in a fog, so I hauled a couple of points to the north and proceeded on my way. Having noted the bearing of the berg, I could continue with the assurance of avoiding it, but how many more were there? Certainly for the hour or two during which it had been clear only this one had been in sight, and I rigidly kept in my mind that the mathematical chances of hitting one must be small.

At noon there is only another 100 miles to go. With the wind backing to N.N.E. the yacht steers herself very steadily with the wind abeam. Every four hours I read the log and reckon how many miles are left. What to do about making the land in this thick fog and possibly a strong wind, I leave for decision until the time comes. It is something of a fence to cross, but I will wait till I come to it, and from a study of the Newfoundland Sailing Directions I have great hopes that the northerly wind will clear away the fog. This occurred at 4 P.M. An hour later I made out several more bergs, one high and the others flat. They lay some miles to the north. The sun appeared for a few moments, and I got a snap at it. The ship was twenty-seven miles astern of the reckoning, but I was none too sure of the time. I have had no sight for latitude for several days, and may be many miles out.

At 8.45 P.M. I hoisted the working staysail in place of the big one, since with dusk coming on it was advisable to have the ship under instant command. The sea was comparatively smooth, so that I did not get wet while working on the forecastle. For a couple of hours longer I remained at the helm, continually peering out into the dark ahead for possible icebergs; then, finding this strict look-out too much of a strain, I hove to under very easy canvas. It was very snug and peaceful in the cabin, and the yacht made hardly any way, the governor wheel of the log not even turning.

Next morning I continued sailing at 5.30 A.M., wind fresh from the north and colder than ever; but I have used up all possible adjectives about the temperature. There is the usual note in my log about the spinnaker boom. This time the bracket aloft had carried away, and the topping lift had chafed through again. I got the spar down on deck, where it could be carried safely, though it is rather in the way.

I had reckoned that I might sight land about noon, and was keeping no very special look-out except for a casual glance ahead now and then for possible icebergs. I cooked a substantial breakfast, ate it, and cleared up in a quite leisurely manner. At 9 A.M. I came on deck and glanced ahead.

LAND! It seemed too good to be true, and I could hardly believe my eyes; but there it was quite definite and unmistakable. A high and rocky coast-line lay ten to fifteen miles ahead with a conspicuous headland running to the north. Never again will it be possible to experience such a thrill as I did then as I gazed at the new continent spread out before me. In my excitement I stood up and patted the rail of the cockpit, shouting endearing names to my ship which had brought me so safely and surely across the ocean to America. Really there, certain and sure, and only a few miles ahead is the new continent, and I have succeeded. Hats off to Red Eric, Columbus, Cabot, and the rest; but this lonely run of mine, with day after day and week after week of nothing but sea around me, made me realise as never before the staunchness and drive of those early explorers, who did not know how far they had to go nor what they had to meet. Only one who has sailed for weeks on end without sighting anything can realise the immensity of the oceans and their loneliness.

But where was I? Obviously that distant shore must be Newfoundland, and that north-running cape is very definite. It should be Cape St. Francis, but might possibly be Bonavista or some even more northerly headland. There was nothing to the southward that could possibly fit in with it. My last latitude was four days ago, and a hasty shot with a poor horizon at that. But don't panic or get too excited; previous landfalls have always been reasonably correct, and so probably is this one. I pored over the brand-new charts and feverishly read the coast description in the Sailing Directions. It all fits in with Cape St. Francis, the point I was aiming at, and again almost too good to be true.

I steered for the headland, gradually becoming more and more certain that it was the right one. Conditions were ideal: a fresh breeze, clear weather, a clean bold coast and my harbour, easy of entrance, well to leeward. Surely now there could be no slip between cup and lip. As I approached the land, the detail of the coastline could be made out; to the southward two prominent headlands showed up which fitted in well with the picture on the chart as Redcliffe Head and the Sugar Loaf. When I was about five miles offshore I bore up confidently to the southward for the entrance to St. John's, then about fifteen miles distant.

But now, lest I should get above myself, my pride had something of a fall. I sailed confidently on until I came to what appeared to be St. John's Bay. When some half-mile from the cliffs I felt suspicious. I could see no harbour entrance nor the lighthouse on Cape Spear, although all the bearings seem to fit in. Something was wrong; I tacked and hove-to, heading seaward while I pored over the chart again. I was in Tor Bay, and St. John's lay six miles farther on. *Emanuel* continued her progress along the coast; to seaward was a small berg, but I was much too impatient to go out of my way for any photographs now. Soon I could make out the lighthouse on the real Cape Spear, and the harbour entrance lay before me clear beyond all doubt. There was a narrow gut between high cliffs, and the wind was going light, so that there might be difficulty in handling the ship under the land. I hove-to again and shook out all the reefs; next, the anchor was got up from below and shackled on to the cable, and I headed for the harbour once more. No pilot came out, nor was one needed, and I sailed into the Narrows. The wind dropped as I had expected, but before the yacht had lost her way came puffs, first on one bow and then on the other. The sheets were trimmed in a moment, and there was ample room for a handy little craft like mine to beat through the Narrows. The harbour then lay before me, with the town to starboard and rugged hill to port. Alongside one of the nearer wharves lay a large cruiser (H.M.S. *Dragon*), while ahead were a number of schooners at anchor. Hailing one, my first words for twenty-four days, I inquired where to anchor, and was told to let go anywhere. Rounding into the wind I let go, and was soon surrounded by a crowd of boats from the schooners. Willing hands stowed my sails and launched the dinghy, and a few minutes later I was towed alongside Messrs. Baird's wharf.

Subsequent worked-out positions on the chart showed that when land was sighted, the ship was sixteen miles north and three miles west of the dead-reckoning positions.

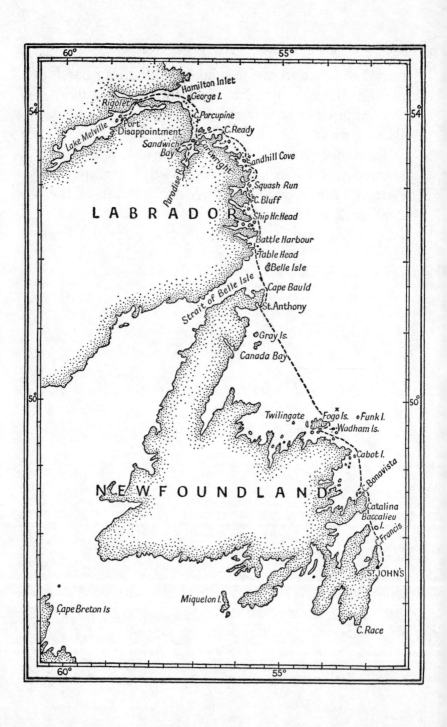

CHAPTER V

NEWFOUNDLAND

NEXT morning an officer from H.M.S. *Dragon* came on board, offering any assistance that might be required and suggesting that I come and lay alongside them. This invitation was readily accepted, and presently the police-launch towed me to the other end of the harbour, where I berthed alongside the wharf under the *Dragon*'s stern. Until her departure several days later I lived on board this warship as a guest of the wardroom.

On one occasion she dressed ship. I borrowed a set of boat's flags, and, with the help of two signalmen, followed motions. In the evening the captain and officers of the *Dragon* gave a dance. *Emanuel* was hauled alongside her gangway, and an illuminating circuit was run over the masthead. Thus equipped, my cabin formed a much sought after sitting-out place. One of the *Dragon*'s officers lent me dress clothes, so that I could attend the dance, where I made many pleasant acquaintances.

After the *Dragon*'s departure I towed up to Messrs. Ayre's wharf, where I remained for the remainder of the fortnight which I spent at St. John's. This fine natural harbour consists of a basin about a mile long and a quarter of a mile broad, connecting with the sea by a narrow channel. This channel, half a mile long, is contracted by rocks to a navigable width of 100 yards. It is adequately buoyed, and presents no difficulty except what may occur from baffling airs when the wind is blowing from the hills, 500 to 600 feet high, which surround the harbour. The town, of which the population is about 50,000, occupies the whole of the northern side of the harbour.

Colonial hospitality is well known, and was extended to me most freely. Many visitors came to see my ship, but the one whom perhaps I was most proud to receive was Captain Bob Bartlett of Arctic fame. He was at the time busy preparing his schooner, the *Morrissey*, for another expedition to the north.

St. John's is one of the few ports of the world where sail is still very much alive, practically all the local carrying trade being done by water in schooners from thirty to two hundred tons. This is the sole rig, in so much so that the word schooner has become synonymous with sailing vessel, and *Emanuel* was often spoken of as 'that little schooner.' They appear to carry a good spread of canvas, not very tall masts, but with long main booms projecting well over the stern. The height of my mast, thirty-four and a half feet from truck to deck, aroused considerable comment. Some of the schooners are fitted with auxiliary engines, when they generally do without their topmasts and carry a leg-of-mutton sail on the main instead of the ordinary gaff sail.

There is a good deal of cultivated ground and meadow around the town, and some of the landscape reminds one very much of England. Elsewhere are either rocky hills or spruce forest. I was taken for a very delightful walk over the hills on the southern side of the harbour to a bay a few miles distant. There seems to be no spring here, but the vegetation had suddenly burst into rapid growth at the beginning of summer—spruce, birch, alder, and many flowers which are not found in England or are represented by different species.

The scents and sights of the countryside were indeed pleasing after nothing but salt water for twenty-four days. Very common is a tiny lily of the valley with minute flowers. Buttercups are common, with many other English weeds, but my great thrill was on coming to a swamp where there were masses of the pitcher plant. They were hardly in flower, but I pulled up a plant showing buds which subsequently opened in my cabin.

I heard a good deal of talk about the new Commission Government. Without entering into politics the general feeling seemed one of gladness at the change and hope for the future.

On 1st July was held the very impressive ceremony of 'Remembrance Day,' conducted by the War Veterans' Association, a body affiliated to the British Legion. It was on this day in 1916 that the Newfoundland Regiment suffered frightful losses on the Somme. After a short service a number of bereaved mothers laid wreaths at the foot of the war memorial. It was impossible for one's eyes to remain quite dry as an elderly working woman approached wearing four sets of medals.

In the afternoon I took some friends for a sail. There was a fresh breeze outside the Narrows necessitating a reef in the mainsail and staysail. We had a very jolly beat back, during which my two companions became quite expert at handling the head-sheets.

I had let it be known in the Press that I should be glad of a companion for a cruise to Labrador. The only offers were: firstly, a young lady from the butcher's shop; and secondly, a rather weedy youth who wanted to sell boot polish on the coast. There is no yacht club at St. John's, neither were there any yachts. I suspect that the Newfoundlanders have so much to do with the sea on business that they do not care to go sailing for pleasure. Neither of the above-mentioned candidates was entirely suitable, so I decided to continue alone.

After waiting for the mail, which contained letters from home, I sailed on the afternoon of 2nd July. Clear of the entrance the wind dropped and

94

left me rolling, becalmed, in the swell. The rocks were close, and for a few minutes I was in some anxiety lest the ship should drift on to them; then an air pulled me clear of the shore, but soon died away again. It was a tiring night, since, being near the shore and with the possibility of traffic, I had to keep on the alert. Now and again a breath of wind would give the yacht steerage way. Morning found the ship five miles east of Cape St. Francis; at 8 A.M. a light south-east air sprang up, and, after rounding the Cape, I steered north for Split Point, passing through the sound between the point and Baccalieu Island. This word, spelt in various ways, means codfish, and has been found connected with Newfoundland at a very early period, giving rise to a suspicion that the Bretons were fishing off these coasts before Cabot's discovery in 1497.

From here I sailed across Trinity Bay, hoping to make Catalina before dark; but, as I approached the land, the wind went very light and headed me. It also got foggy. I could see dimly a headland, some outlying rocks, and the occasional glare of the light on Green Island. For an hour or so I tacked slowly to windward, hardly making any progress and getting more and more sleepy. The prospect of reaching harbour seemed remote, so I stood in to the land till I got soundings and let go off Melrose. In this open anchorage the yacht rolled heavily, but this did not prevent my sleeping. If the wind came onshore I could count on the changed motion to awake me. Next morning on my way in to Catalina I hailed a passing fisherman for directions. 'Straight ahead through the tickle,' he replied. I had learned the language and realised that the 'tickle' meant the sound between Green Island and the main. Many of the sounds are so narrow that the rocks may tickle the sides of a passing ship; at least that was the explanation of the term that was given me.

This particular tickle was deep and clear. After passing through it I sailed up the western arm and anchored off Port Union.

The jaws of the gaff were still giving trouble in spite of the leather and quantities of grease, so I decided to put a sheet of copper round the mast to take the chafe, but no such sheet could be found ashore. A half-built schooner on the stocks was an object of some interest. She would be of about seventy tons, showed fine lines with plenty of dead rise, and should sail well. She was very heavily built of local wood, except for the planking, which was of Canadian fir. The workmanship was rough.

Returning to the yacht I had a visit from the crew of a fishing schooner. They suggested that I might find a sheet of copper at Catalina village on the opposite side of the harbour, and took a great delight in hoisting my sails and helping me to sail over there. Again, no copper sheet could be found, but eventually a tinsmith was unearthed who provided me with a piece of thin galvanised iron which would serve the purpose equally well.

Several more schooners were waiting in the harbour for suitable weather to proceed to Labrador. I had tea, which included fried fish, on board one of them, the *Alma Francis*. The meal was preceded by a grace. It was a bit crowded in her tiny forecastle with her crew of six men, but they made me very much at home, and I stopped for a long time talking shop. *Emanuel* was very much admired, and they were very appreciative of my trip across the Atlantic. After the twenty-four days of solitude I still had arrears of chattering to make up.

My next port was Bonavista, a town of some 5,000 inhabitants, and the largest 'outport,' as the settlements outside St. John's are called. A whole host of new impressions were here stamped on my mind. One evening I was taken to see a cod-trap hauled. This is a square net moored to the bottom, one side being extended as a leader to within a short distance of the shore. The fish, encountering the leader, swim into the net and cannot find their way out. When being hauled, the net is first closed by a rope and then brought slowly to the surface. A solid mass of cod appeared, which were scooped up in a hand-net and thrown into the boat, after which the trap was lowered to the bottom again. About half a ton of cod was secured, and also a twelve-pound salmon, which latter was presented to me. The traps are hauled twice a day.

I had a letter of introduction to Mr. Rousel, the local magistrate. He, unfortunately, was away, but his wife welcomed me very warmly. I also made the acquaintance of Dr. Forbes, who, with his charming family, made me much at home and asked me up to his house for several meals.

Dr. Forbes took me round the town, and his daughter helped me to take photographs. The most interesting sight was the capelin coming ashore. Thess are small fish about the size of a sardine, which during certain weeks in the summer swim up to the beach in countless millions. Some are thrown up by the surf; many more are hauled in by means of nets cast from the shore. This coming in of the capelin is part of the reproductive cycle. The fishermen believe that two males place themselves one on each side of the female. As they are rolled on to the beach they press her sides and the spawn is ejected. Certainly the whole beach is bestrewn with spawn as well as with fish. The latter are carted away by the ton, and either spread out to dry or used as manure. When dried, they are used for winter dog-feed as well as for human consumption.

Dogs are important as they provide the only means of transport during the winter except for the railway. In summer they help to pull small carts, and the children drive round selling cods' tongues. I never knew that a cod had a tongue, and thought that I was being made fun of when told this, but, as a matter of fact, they are considered a delicacy and taste very good, something like a sweetbread with a slight fishy flavour.

The dogs themselves are rather a mongrel type, as the true husky, which I saw later in Labrador, is not permitted in Newfoundland. Huskies, which are hardly differentiated from wolves, are so fierce that no domestic animals can be kept in their neighbourhood. They cannot bark, but can only howl like wolves.

Fishing is the only industry in the place, and practically everyone is occupied with it or its by-products. The cod are split and cleaned directly they are brought ashore. This is done on covered stages called 'flakes,' built of poles and projecting out over the sea so that the offal can drop through into the water. The fish are then put into tubs with salt and later spread out to dry. The men work very hard night and day, with only two or three hours' rest, when the fish are running, but Dr. Forbes remarked that Newfoundland was the only country where a man had to work for only three months during the year. In the winter they build boats, repair nets, and cut firewood from the neighbouring forests, but I suspect that with many the time hangs heavily during the winter with its long nights and frozen ground. Melancholic insanity is not uncommon.

We drove out in Dr. Forbes's car to the lighthouse on Cape Bonavista. This is claimed, without, I fancy, much foundation, to be Cabot's landfall. After crossing the Atlantic myself it is perhaps not too presumptuous to imagine that I can enter into the feelings of the early explorers. What a thrill that must have been when land was reported, and what would one not give for a detailed log by Cabot; but he probably never kept one.

Only two types of boats seem common, one the well-known flat-bottomed dory, and the other the trap skiff, a powerful, narrow, open motor-boat about thirty feet long. Sails have been almost discarded for boats. The dories have a great name for seaworthiness. I do not think it is warranted; their safety lies in the expert manner in which they are handled. Their merit is due to their being very light and cheap to build, and also to the fact that they can be stowed one inside the other. Having a flat bottom and no keel they could not possibly sail on a wind, but their lightness must make them very buoyant in a seaway. It is on record that a dory has sailed from America to England. There is no regular boat-building industry in Newfoundland, since the fishermen usually build their own boats, and often their own schooners.

The town of Bonavista consists of a collection of wooden houses, some churches, a few stores, and a cod-liver-oil factory. Outside the town are a few meadows, but no real agriculture can be carried on, since corn will not ripen. Beyond the meadows lies waste, rocky, or marshy ground for some miles, and then forest.

I set sail during the early afternoon of 7th July and made a good and enjoyable run across the open water at the mouth of Bonavista Bay. The wind was just too fresh to carry the spinnaker, and I had the mortification of being overtaken by a schooner. By 10 P.M., when it was dark, I was a couple of miles off Cabot Island, which is situated six miles from the headland of Cape Freels. Between this island and the shore are numerous islets and rocks, some of which, including Cabot Island itself, are lit.

The south-west wind freshened, and the glass was falling, so that it was necessary to heave to and reef; dense fog came on at the same time, blotting out all lights. I carried on steering north-east so as to give a wide berth to two sunken rocks, but at 11.40 P.M., as it was still too thick to make the next light (Gull I.), I hove to for a spell. At midnight further reduction of sail was required, the staysail being reefed and a third roll put in the mainsail. There was not much sea, and my only anxiety was lest the wind should back to the south-east, when the yacht would have been in an awkward position with a fringe of rocky islets to leeward. At 1.20 A.M. the glass had steadied, and after the one and a half hour's rest I was ready to take the helm again. I could safely run some miles to the north-west and still be in no worse position, so I let draw and continued on that course. A couple of hours later the wind veered west and went light.

It was a wonderful dawn, the sky all shades of red and pink with a low-lying bank of fog to leeward. As the sun rose the fog dried up and disclosed a gigantic berg a mile on the lee bow. The top of it was fretted into curiously shaped cliffs, and must have been several hundred feet high. When first sighted it was not fully light, and I imagined the dark shape to be a cloud; but its outline remained constant, and with full daylight it took on its characteristic vivid white colour.

It was some hours before the yacht's position could be ascertained, but after a time I sighted the Wadham Islands, and just fetched between Upper Wadham and Small Island at 10.40 A.M. This passage appears clear except for Tom Cod Rock and South-South-West Rock, which are both well shown by breakers. I was some ten to twelve miles

behind the reckoning, and could not imagine
where I had been sailing all night. Strong tide or
currents are not very probable on this coast, and
presumably my record of courses while manœuvring or hove-to off Cabot Island must have been
incorrect.

The wind was now dead ahead for Fogo Island,
and for almost the first time since leaving England
I found myself beating to windward. At 3 p.m. I
was off Cape Fogo, having made ten miles in the
last five hours. Two miles per hour is about as
much as *Emanuel* can hope to make good against
the wind. The wind, now, was very variable,
blowing at times with strong squalls which required reefs, and at other times dying almost to
calm. A small but steep chop checked my progress;
for a time I debated whether to seek anchorage in
a nameless bay just south of Tilting Harbour, but
a puff of wind with some east in it made it seem
probable that I could sail the course under the
lee of the land to 'Seldom Come By' (what a name!).
The idea of a secure anchorage prevailed, and I
sailed along the south-west coast of Fogo, enjoying
the scent of the pine-trees from the land. One or
two lulls made me fearful of having to spend another night at sea, but at 6 a.m. I managed to make
the harbour, and came to in very snug quarters off
the wharf on the north-west arm.

The next day was very cold with a hard north

wind, so that sailing did not seem very attractive. I
was glad of a quiet morning to write up the log.
In the afternoon I walked some miles along the
rough track leading to Fogo village on the other
side of the island. From this path some winters
before, the local clergyman had lost his way and
been frozen to death. It was a lovely undulating
country, thickly covered with scrub of birch and
spruce. In the open swampy patches the dull-red
flowers of the pitcher plant were conspicuous;
Labrador tea made a showy display with its heads
of small white flowers. Chlodora and a purplish
flower akin to an azalea were common, as well as
the large flower of the tiny crackerberry. As usual
in Newfoundland, one could not walk far without
coming on 'ponds,' as the lakes are called, and
very lovely they looked among the tree-covered
vistas.

On my return I spent some time chatting with
the local inhabitants on the wharf, and was then
invited aboard the schooner *Young Hood* which lay
alongside. She was a trading ship of 200 tons
with a roomy, well-kept, and tidy forecastle in
which we took tea. She carried salt, which she was
distributing to the fishermen in the district. Her
skipper had served in the Navy through the War,
and we had an interesting talk over old times.
There are no social distinctions in Newfoundland,
and I gathered that he found life on the lower deck

puzzling at first; but he soon tumbled to the Naval routine and appeared to retain very friendly memories of the Service.

It seems to be generally regretted that the Newfoundland Naval Reserve has been discontinued. In view of the approaching increases in the Navy it is to be hoped that this service may be started again.

The following day the wind was favourable, and I continued on my way northward. After rounding Fogo Island I had to find my way through the long reef of rocks and islands which lie some miles to the northward. From the chart the best passage looked to be between Little Fogo and Bishop Islands. This is a clear sound half a mile wide, but there are extensive shoals around the latter. It was easy enough to avoid them by keeping on the correct bearings, but at the same time rather disconcerting to notice the sea suddenly break a few hundred yards on the bow even though one knew that there were rocks underneath the water in that position.

Once clear of the reef I set course for St. Anthony, rather more than 100 miles distant. It was an ideal sailing day with the wind just before the beam, a bright sun, and smooth sea. Towards the evening an iceberg was sighted ahead. It was difficult to make any estimate of its distance, and consequently I had to keep on the alert during the dark hours. About midnight there was a striking case of abnormal refraction, Bacalhao Light (another variant of the spelling) being sighted when about fifty miles distant.

At daylight Gray Islands were visible ahead, but with a light wind it required the whole day to pass them. A tiresome swell made it difficult to keep the ship on her course. As the mainland showed up I noticed white patches on the hills; a long row of houses at first seemed the most likely explanation, but the distance was too great for that; perhaps smoke from a train, until I remembered that there was no railway within some hundreds of miles; nor could it be patches of mist, since the outline remained constant, so I let it go as one of the world's mysteries. After anchoring, some patches of snow on the hills afforded the rather obvious explanation, but I had not thought of snow in July.

At dusk *Emanuel* was off Hare Bay with St. Anthony Light in sight, but progress was provokingly slow, and I felt tired after a sleepless night. The wind freshened from off the land, and the yacht was soon sailing under jib and close-reefed main. About midnight I had worked up close to the land, and against my better judgment I decided to locate the narrow entrance to the harbour and to see what it looked like in the dark. I first hove to, got the anchor ready, and all prepared for anchoring; the wind was now strong with really fierce squalls blowing off the cliffs. The fixed light at the entrance showed up, and I made out the passage looking rather like the mouth of a huge cave, while the land a mile away on the far side of St. Mein Bay was clearly visible as a black shadow on the horizon. I first reached well up into the latter and past the narrows; putting about, I left the jib aback while I made the final preparations for anchoring and then let draw for the entrance. Tacking under the fixed light, a very heavy squall struck the ship, and as I hauled in the jib-sheet I had the sickening feeling of the rope coming in without resistance. Clearly something had parted, but the noise of the surf and the slatting of the mainsail drowned the flapping of the jib. I tugged madly on the furling line, and was able partially to roll up the sail, and then jumped forward to hoist the staysail, which should previously have been reefed, but was not. Long streamers of torn canvas flapped wildly from the jib, and I had to be careful to avoid the staysail-sheet blocks which shook across the deck with angry violence. There was no time to get the halyards really taut, much less to coil down and clear up the tangle forward, and I sprang back to the helm and seized the staysail-sheet to steady in the sail before it tore to rags like the jib. The rocks were close to leeward; there seemed no hope of

staying with my reduced mainsail and half the jib
flapping loose from the bowsprit; anyway, instant
decision was vital (I like to think and talk all
round a subject, and then ask someone else's
advice before I act). There seemed room to wear
round, so I put the helm hard up and let fly the
main-sheet. Round she came, heading seaward,
when to my surprise and horror she struck.
Bump, bump, and again, bump, as the iron keel
crashed heavily on what was evidently hard rock.
'Here's the end of the cruise' flashed through my
mind, but after the third bump the yacht gathered
way and answered her helm. Clear, but at what cost,
and where could I beach her? As the mainsail
gybed over, the peak purchase came adrift from
its cleat. I could not tell at the time what was wrong,
except that the gaff dropped right down. One
damned thing after another, as is always the way
at sea. There was no time to look at the chart, and
anyway I was pretty sure that no sandy beach lay
in reach. Will it be quicker to cut the dinghy's
lashings or untie them? Probably the latter, since
my knife has not been recently sharpened. I shone
my torch on the cabin floor. No sign of water yet.
Can it be possible that *Emanuel's* luck has held
and that she is undamaged? I steered out to sea,
and after running for a mile to get clear of the
land I hove-to. Then came the business of clearing
up the mess. The peak purchase had come unrove,

but I was able to hoist the sail pretty well on the halyards; then down staysail and reef while the ship ranged wildly without any headsail to balance her, but the water was smooth under the lee of the land. It was very dark, except occasionally when the northern lights gleamed in the sky. Then two more rolls in the mainsail, and the ship was under control and properly hove-to. After hot coffee and a glass of rum I was ready to continue clearing up forward. The jib-sheets had to be refitted, and the old sail, which had torn away from the clew, stowed below. The storm-jib was set in its place, and the tangle of wet ropes coiled down. By the time everything was ship-shape again it was getting light, and I let draw for the harbour entrance. It was blowing a full gale, but under her reduced canvas *Emanuel* handled readily, and stayed each time without hesitation. The entrance is about 200 yards wide, and a great number of tacks were required before I got through the narrows. I dropped anchor at the head of the harbour at 4.45 A.M. after being on the go for nearly forty-eight hours. I was glad enough to turn in, though by no means utterly exhausted.

I awoke after a few hours' sleep to find the cabin floor awash; rather alarming, though the pump sucked after a few minutes' work, showing that the water was not coming in very fast. Evidently the jar of striking the rocks the previous night had caused a small leak, but there seemed no immediate danger of the ship sinking.

The harbour of St. Anthony consists of a narrow, land-locked basin one and a half miles long, and surrounded by low hills. The main village lies on the lower slopes of the southern shore, and consists of the usual collection of small wooden houses. Adjoining the village are the buildings of the Grenfell Mission. Except for some wooded areas on the slopes, the hills are covered by rough scrub, alternating with patches of bare rock. Numerous wooden jetties project from the shore, which is all rocky. Sandy beaches seem entirely absent from Newfoundland.

I remained at St. Anthony for a fortnight, enjoying the hospitality of my relative, Sir Wilfred Grenfell. I had not previously had the honour of meeting him, but after calling on him and explaining the rather intricate family connection, he invited me to stay with him while I remained at St. Anthony. I also presented a letter of introduction to Mr. Moore, the chief merchant of the neighbourhood, and spent several pleasant evenings with his family.

It was most interesting to see something of the work of the Mission, hospital, orphanage, school, dockyard, &c. For a few days I actually became a 'missionary' myself, being put in charge of the eighty-ton Mission steam yacht, *Strathcona II*, for a trip to Canada Bay and Twilingate. I had a crew of two 'wops' (college boys working voluntarily for the Mission), Abe Mercer as pilot, and Will Styles as engineer. After calling at Canada Bay, Abe seemed rather alarmed at my setting a course direct for Twilingate some eighty miles away, instead of coasting from headland to headland. I acquired a somewhat undeserved reputation as a navigator when our port showed up right ahead. Miss Kivimaki accompanied us to inspect the books of the Canada Bay sawmills.

During my stay *Emanuel* was hauled up on the Mission slip, and after poking about for some time water trickled out from one of the garboard seams. The caulking was found decayed under the paint. One of the chain plates was found to be fractured just below the channels. It looked like a long-standing crack, and if I sailed across the Atlantic with it I am glad that I did not know it.

I was interested in being shown round the extensive Mission gardens. A rotary cultivator was at work, probably the only one in Newfoundland. Turnips and potatoes were doing well, and lettuce and radishes can be grown. Early varieties are chosen on account of the short growing season. In the greenhouses tomatoes were ripening well, and there was a very fine show of flowers. A few apple-trees had been planted outside, but had died back badly, probably from the severe winter frosts, but they were now making vigorous growth.

When *Emanuel's* refit was complete, a party, consisting of the Moores and Miss Large, sailed with me to Cremaillere Bay for a picnic. The French place-names are a legacy from the time when that nation occupied these shores.

CHAPTER VI

LABRADOR

LABRADOR, whither I was now bound, merits a few words of description. The coast-line is much broken and is generally fringed by a chain of rocky islands. Deep bays run into the land, the largest of which, Hamilton Inlet, opens into Lake Melville, seventy-five miles long and seventeen miles wide. The outer fringe is indescribably barren, but away from the sea the lower slopes of the hills are mostly covered by spruce forest. Here and there patches of beech, poplar, and other deciduous trees lighten the general rather dark and gloomy tone of the fir-trees. Above the trees are barren grey-green wastes of reindeer moss. To some extent one is reminded of the west coast of Scotland; but in Labrador, at least in the southern part which I visited, the hills are much lower and more rounded, generally rising to only 400 or 500 feet.

The country is entirely unchanged by man. There are, perhaps, 3,000 permanent settlers of European extraction, mostly descendants of servants of the Hudson Bay Company who remained in the country after their period of service had expired. A few hundred Eskimos live in settlements northward from Hamilton Inlet. Some scattered tribes of Indians roam the interior, coming out to the coast once a year to barter their furs. The permanent settlers, 'livieres' as they are called ('because they live 'ere'), have winter homes at the head of the bays, from which the men go some hundreds of miles into the interior trapping furs. In the spring the river mouths are netted for salmon, and later they move to the outer coasts for the cod fishery. During the summer some 10,000 fishermen, mostly from Newfoundland, come to the coast after the cod. Some fish from their schooners; others bring their boats up by steamer and camp ashore in rough huts. Many of the crews, either in the schooners or camping ashore, bring a girl with them to do the cooking.

The summer climate is pleasant enough, comparable to a cool English summer, but the winter is fully arctic. The land lies under deep snow, and the sea is frozen until the following May or June.

Except for wandering bands of Indians, the interior is entirely uninhabited. None of it is properly mapped, and much is still even unexplored. Only some two or three travellers have ever crossed from the Atlantic coast to the shores of Hudson Bay.

Southward from Cartwright the coast has been adequately charted. An echo of the controversy between Canada and Newfoundland is to be found in the excellent chart of Lake Melville, made by the Government of the former, and which is headed 'Canada, East Coast.' The decision of the Privy Council put the boundary at the 'height of the land,' several hundred miles from the coast.

The 'livieres' are all desperately poor and permanently in debt to the merchants. The truck system, by which the merchants supply outfits and take the furs and fish in exchange, has been sufficiently described in the report of the Royal Commission which, a couple of years ago, visited Newfoundland. That the system is a bad one can be readily admitted, but blame cannot be attributed to individuals.

The 'livieres' have intermarried to a considerable extent with the Indians and Eskimos. There is no evidence that this racial mixture leads to any degeneration. There is an entire absence of any class or race feeling, so that children of mixed blood incur no social drawbacks. It is a hard life for the men, but they live an active life and are their own masters. For the women it is not so good, confined, as they may be, to their houses for most of the winter.

In former days there were no doctors, schools, nor other social services. In 1892 Dr. Grenfell (later Sir Wilfred) visited Labrador in a ship belonging to the Mission to the Deep Sea Fishermen.

He was so shocked by the hardships under which the people lived, and by the terrible suffering caused by the lack of medical attention, that he has devoted his life to remedying the conditions under which the people lived. He has largely succeeded, and the work of the International Grenfell Association is well known. I do not feel competent to give an adequate account of the Mission and its work, and it would be presumption on my part to attempt to portray this great man, but, walking through the wards of the hospital at St. Anthony one is very conscious of the immense amount of sheer physical suffering that Grenfell has been instrumental in relieving. Along the coast one is constantly struck by personal devotion which he has inspired among the common folk. One man who had served for many years in the Mission ships said that life would hardly be worth living when the 'doctor' was no longer with them.[1]

On 26th July, after a false start owing to a calm, I sailed at 2.25 P.M. before a light south-west air. There was a fine iceberg off French Point, a few miles down the coast, and I sailed close round it taking photographs. I noticed no decrease in tem-

[1] Anyone wishing for further information about the Grenfell Mission should write to the Secretary, I.G.A., 66 Victoria Street, London, S.W.1. There are usually vacancies for voluntary summer workers of either sex, and a number of college boys and girls spend their vacation working for the Mission as boats' crews, secretaries, &c.

perature while in its vicinity. Then proceeding slowly along the rugged coast I came to St. Lunaire Bay, and sailed for about a mile up a delightful little inlet on the southern corner of the bay. It was quite uninhabited, and I felt I had all the world to myself.

I weighed anchor next morning at 8.15 A.M.; good time, since breakfast and preparing for sea takes quite two hours. I carried a light fair wind as far as Cape Bauld. This is the north-east extremity of Newfoundland, and has a lighthouse on it. Here the wind dropped, and *Emanuel* rolled helplessly for an hour or so; but at 2 p.m. a fresh north-west wind made, and the yacht began to show her paces. I could just lay the course for Cape Charles across Belle Isle Straits. There was a slight sea, and some spray came on board, but the leak seemed to have been stopped effectually. The wind increased, so that reefs had to be taken in. Presently I was off Belle Isle, a high, barren island surrounded by forbidding cliffs. There were several steamers in sight, and I realised that I was crossing one of the great shipways of the world.

As I neared the Labrador shore the wind went light. I sailed past Table Head, White Mica Cove, with Camp Island just ahead, eagerly taking in the details of this new continent. It appeared a black, barren land, but the outlines of the rocky hills were rounded by glacial action. A big rock on the top of a hill was probably a boulder dropped by the retreating ice. In 'Main Tickle' the wind dropped, and I drifted through into Niger Sound as the light died away. It was not a very inviting prospect. The best anchorage lay under an island a couple of miles away, but it would be difficult to make my way to it in the dark. To the left and near at hand appeared a cleft in the rocks with boats at anchor, evidently the sound between Deer Island and the mainland; but the scale of my chart was too small to show any detail, and there was only a line of unhelpful reference in the Sailing Directions.

I got out the sweep and began to row *Emanuel* towards the boats. Soon it was quite dark, but the loom of the high cliffs on each side was visible. Then a breath of air blew down the sound and filled the sails. With my heart in my mouth I tacked slowly up in the direction in which I had seen the boats. Not until I was right among them and within a stone's-throw of the shore could I get soundings and let go the anchor. The swell growled sullenly on the pebbly beach, and I wondered where I had got to. Presently a moving lantern shone out on shore, and I hailed to know if I was in a safe anchorage. The reply was inaudible, but after a few minutes a couple of fishermen rowed out. Friendly and helpful as these Newfoundland fishermen always are, they towed me across to the schooner anchorage on the other side of the sound, which they called Chimney Tickle.

Next morning there was a light head-wind, and I could only make slow progress. After rounding Cape Charles, I sailed through Caribou Channel, following a pencil line which one of the schooner captains had drawn for me on the chart. This is a winding passage a few hundred yards wide between various bleak and rocky islets at the back of Great Caribou Island. Two sunken rocks were buoyed by small white sticks with flags on them, and an unwatched light-beacon marked the northern end. It seemed rather strange to find navigational marks in such a desolate country, but there is a great deal of schooner traffic on the coast. As I could barely make headway against the slight adverse current, I anchored in a cove for lunch. Proceeding later I drifted into Battle Harbour. This, best described as a ditch between two rocks, is one of the principal settlements of Labrador, and consists of perhaps twenty houses and a store.

Emanuel, as usual, was the centre of interest to the local fishermen. They had all heard of my voyage across the Atlantic, and my answer to the usual run of questions became almost automatic.

The wind went round to the south during the night, and I awoke to find a good fresh breeze. The previous evening there had been some talk of

a walk with Miss Loveridge, to whose father I had
brought a letter of introduction, but this fair wind
was too good to waste. (This last sentence is awk-
wardly expressed. If Miss Loveridge should ever
read these lines I assure her that a walk would
have been no waste of time; but I was anxious to
get north, and the engagement had only been
provisional on my being held up by contrary
winds.) There was not room to handle the yacht,
so I ran out under staysail and set the mainsail
outside.

With the big staysail boomed out, *Emanuel* ran
down the coast from headland to headland, making a steady five knots through the fairly smooth
sea. Cape St. Lewis, Spear Point, Cape St. Francis,
Ship Harbour Head, and Cape Bluff were some
of the names, and each presented an iron-bound
appearance, dark cliffs, and rocky shore. Between
them were great bays running out of sight fifteen
or twenty miles into the land. There was an intri-
guing lack of detail about them on the chart, and
I hoped to explore some of them on my way back.
After passing Cape Bluff a little before 4 P.M., I
was able to take an inside run, and sailed for the
next fifteen miles at the back of a chain of islands.
The last part of the passage, called Squasho Run,
is a narrow sound, five or six miles long, and rather
reminds one of the Sound of Mull, though the
hills are not nearly so high. The lower shores of

Squasho are well wooded, and form a pleasing contrast to the bleak desolation of the outer coast.

Emerging from the end of this sound, it was time to seek anchorage for the night. Ahead of me the chart showed an unnamed cove which looked sheltered. Sounding carefully, I sailed in and let go. A stream ran into the head of the cove, connecting with a lake a quarter of a mile inland. I took my rod ashore and cast a fly here and there, but without result. After supper I rowed about the cove examining the bottom. The rocky cliffs and tree-covered slopes looked wild indeed. *Emanuel* anchored in the middle, and, reflected in the smooth water, made a delightful picture, reminding me very vividly of the quotation, 'Lone keels off headlands drear.' This cove is not to be recommended as an anchorage. There is a large boulder which shows at low water on the west side; the entrance is very narrow, and the head of the cove is shallow with a rocky bottom. It is situated two miles west of Big Island in Caplin Bay.

I found myself in rather a tight corner next morning, as there was not much room to get up the anchor and beat out single-handed. To get enough way on to handle the ship I had to stand on till my bowsprit almost overhung the beach, but from my examination of the previous evening I knew where the shallow water lay, and got clear without mishap. I still had the pencilled course on my chart, and so sailed confidently through the narrow channels between Big Island and the main. The scale of my chart was about half an inch to the mile. This is good enough to show the general lie of the coast and to distinguish the different islands, but too small to give much detail of the intricate channels between them. On this coast, drawing only five feet, one can very nearly sail wherever one can see water. Outside the islands there is usually a swell, which breaks on anything under a fathom.

As I drew out to open sea, rain and thick weather set in, and it seemed advisable to avoid the next inside passage. Accordingly, the patent log was streamed and compass courses steered. For the next few hours I sailed along the coast, just sighting the outside rocks. Then, clearing, Domino Run with its lighthouse showed up ahead. It was very pleasant to see a lighthouse again, to know that there really were other people in the world. A little later I passed a group of seven fishing-schooners at anchor with numerous boats moving about between them. They seemed to be embarking salt from a bigger schooner, which was obviously a trader and not a fisherman. I carried on through the run, which is half a mile wide and about five miles long, then outside Indian Island towards Sand Hill Cove. Here the wind veered ahead, and seemed inclined to fall light. For a time

I had barely steerage way, and I lay watching the
forest of masts that appeared ahead in Sand Hill
Cove. Then the wind came again, and I tacked up
towards the anchored fleet. It was not likely that
any of the crews had ever seen an English yacht,
nor one of any other country for that matter, so I
picked my way through the fleet, going as close as
I could to each ship. Really I suppose it was just
showing off, though I did need directions for
anchoring. After I had let go and stowed the sails,
several of their boats came alongside asking if I had
anything to sell. At first I did not understand what
was meant, but it soon appeared that they had
taken *Emanuel* for a rum-runner. The Newfoundland Government have a rather complicated
system of drink restriction in force. I never succeeded in understanding it, but there seems no
retail sale of alcohol, and in practice the fishermen
find it very difficult to get any liquor. Very cheap
drink can be obtained from the French Islands, St.
Pierre and Miquelon, and there is said to be some
illicit traffic on the coast. I saw no signs of it. I am
not myself a teetotaller, but from the tales I heard
from Sir Wilfred of the havoc which drink has
caused on this coast it seems wise that some restriction should be enforced. Sir Wilfred had even
extracted from me a promise that I would not offer
the fishermen drinks. My visitors were not unduly
disappointed at finding *Emanuel* dry, and I spent

a pleasant evening listening to their talk about their life and work on the coast.

It was calm the next morning, so I availed my-self of an invitation to dinner with the captain of the schooner, *A. & E. Butt*. We dined in the after-cabin, being waited on by the girl cook, a niece of the captain. There was a clean tablecloth and a spotless apron in my honour. After our meal the wind sprang up, so that I was able to make good another twenty miles on my way. I anchored in Isthmus Bay, a sheet of water several miles long protected by the usual fringe of islands. The land here is lower, and shoreward there was a wide sweep of rolling tree-covered country. The bay was entirely deserted. I remember sitting at the head of the cabin stairs watching a fine display of the northern lights. Flickering spears of light seemed to converge to the northern horizon.

There is a second entrance to Isthmus Bay through a sound fifty yards wide that goes by the delightful name of Pinch Gut Tickle. This would save me several miles, so I sailed through it, avoiding one rock that was mentioned in the Sail-ing Directions and over the top, as I was told later, of one that is not. This inland navigation probably sounds more perilous than was actually the case. I never got ashore, and was not conscious of taking risks. From Pinch Gut I proceeded along the coast to Cartwright at the mouth of Sandwich Bay.

Cartwright, one of the principal settlements in Labrador, and now a village of 200 or 300 inhabitants, has a history. About 150 years ago a Major Cartwright established a trading and fishing station here which might have been a commercial success had it not been pillaged by American privateers. The village is situated on the northern side of a small bay which opens on to the strait leading to Sandwich Bay. There is a substantial wooden wharf, at the head of which rise the conspicuous buildings of the Hudson Bay Company store. On the other side of the bay, and closely surrounded by woods, are the houses, school, and hospital of the Grenfell Mission. The last was only a ruin owing to a recent fire.

Emanuel must have presented a pretty and unusual picture as she came sailing into the bay with her topsail set, and I noticed quite a crowd of people watching from the shore.

I remained in the vicinity of Cartwright for about a week, being entertained by Mr. Blackhall, manager of the Hudson Bay Company post, and by members of the Grenfell Mission. The latter was under the charge of Dr. Kennard of Boston, U.S.A., assisted by Miss Eveline Hillier as head nurse and housekeeper and by three 'wops.'[1] Some sailing parties were arranged, of which the most

[1] The voluntary Mission workers have assumed with pride this originally somewhat uncomplimentary term.

interesting was an expedition to the head of Sandwich Bay. On this excursion Robbins and John, two of the 'wops,' accompanied me. A narrow sound, six miles long, connects with Sandwich Bay, the latter a fine sheet of inland water eighteen miles across. Sailing one day after lunch we made some progress through the sound until the wind dropped and the tide turned, forcing us to anchor for the night in Muddy Bay. Proceeding early next morning we had a fine sail across the bay, beating against a fresh breeze. The chart gave no details of the passage into Eagle River, whither we were bound, and the verbal directions which had been given me by Mr. Bird of the I.G.A. were not very definite. The houses at Dove Cove were distinguished easily enough (one of Mr. Bird's marks), and I worked up towards them. When about one and a half miles distant from the shore the soundings became very irregular. After suddenly getting two fathoms, it seemed risky to continue without a pilot. With the fresh breeze *Emanuel* was sailing fast, and we might have struck the ground hard enough to incur damage. Accordingly, the anchor was let go, and Robbins and I manned the dinghy to pull ashore and bring out the pilot to whom we had been recommended by Mr. Blackhall. Against the fresh breeze and appreciable current we could make no headway, so I put Robbins back on board. With the dinghy thus lightened I thought I could just make it, as was the case after an hour and a half's real hard rowing. Landing on Separation Point, I walked along the coast for half a mile until I came to a couple of houses and found Mr. Billy Brown, the pilot. At first he said that he was not used to sails, and could not bring *Emanuel* in against the wind, though we might be able to reach White Bear River on the northern side of Separation Point. So off we went in his motor-boat, a powerful craft nearly as long as *Emanuel* and with a seven-horse-power engine. When he realised how small the yacht was, he readily agreed to tow us in, and we anchored abreast his wharf just inside the mouth of the river. Later we went some five or six miles up the river in Mr. Brown's boat and fished, one decent-sized trout being obtained.

Mr. Brown came off to us early next morning to take us up White Bear River on another fishing excursion. We proceeded for some six miles in the motor-boat, and then as it became shallow took to the dinghy for another mile. At first the river is a mile wide, but then it contracts and winds prettily among the tree-covered slopes of the hills. Except for a few houses at the mouth, it is entirely wild.

Major Cartwright gave it its name from the fact of his shooting six polar bears in the vicinity. We landed on a spit of sand, and walked for a quarter of a mile along a rough trail through the forest; then, suddenly emerging from the trees, the falls lay in front of us. They are a grand sight. The Sailing Directions give the height as eighty feet, but the water pours down in two steps. The roar was very impressive. We caught one salmon and one trout, the latter falling to my rod. It was not a very large bag, but I had the excitement of landing a fish for the first time.

Our guide, Mr. Brown, was a most charming man, with the lean, spare appearance of a movie hero and a soft Devon speech underlying the Newfoundland manner of talking. His tales of his winter trapping under real Arctic conditions were most interesting. His round is 150 miles long, and takes five weeks hauling a sledge or 'komatik,' as they are called here. He prefers to go by himself, taking a small cotton tent and iron stove. Being in a forest country there is always wood for fuel, and they can always get rabbits (the Arctic hare) and partridge (ptarmigan). He was inclined to make light of the hardships; certainly casualties among the trappers are very rare, and obviously it is a matter of understanding the conditions. Before the snow becomes fit for sledge travel he packs his gear on his back, and he admitted that a fifteen-mile march carrying 100 pounds was a hard day's work. Dogs are used for hauling firewood and for various other purposes through the winter, but are not taken on the trapping expeditions, as they are too much trouble to look after.

Arriving back at the river mouth, my two companions were discharged to the Mission scow which had come over to load timber. I then sailed to Paradise River at the other corner of the bay some fifteen miles away. Mr. Brown had told me that it was a 'good' river with no shoals, though there is a rocky islet off the south shore at the entrance. I anchored a mile within the mouth, passing several houses on each side of the bank. They were all empty, the inhabitants having moved out to the coast for the cod fishery.

Some five miles from its mouth the Paradise River opens into a lake, against which the chart has the remark, 'Large Lake abounding in Salmon, Trout, and Pike.' Next morning I took my rod and rowed up to find this lake. After a couple of hours' hard pulling against the current I came to rapids. By keeping close into the bank and scrambling, sometimes waist-deep, from stone to stone, it was possible to force or drag the dinghy to the top. I tried casting from the bank in several places and also trolling, but got no fish. There had been plenty of the wet shirt coming up the rapids. These presented a very fine sight with high curling waves which roared angrily. In a canoe it might have been possible to shoot down, but it would have been much too dangerous to attempt in my dinghy, especially as I was quite lacking in that sort of experience.

On my return to Cartwright I found quite a busy scene. The Mission schooner *Cluet* had come in with stores, and the auxiliary motor-yacht *Maraval*, with Dr. Paddon on board, had arrived from the North-West River Settlement. This latter settlement at the head of Lake Melville is the farthest post of the Grenfell Mission. I found myself among a very pleasant little community of Mission workers. Miss Hillier, whom we christened 'Miss Cold as Cartwright' after the reported exclamation of a 'wop' present during the previous summer, added to the gaiety of the party. It was no business of mine to ascertain if this nickname was justified.

It was now necessary to make some plans for the future. I had originally hoped to get as far as Nain, 250 miles farther north. This is the headquarters of the Moravian Mission to the Eskimos; but the stretch of water beyond Hamilton Inlet is practically uncharted, and I realised that it would be incurring too grave a risk to sail without a pilot. The account of North-West River, with its gardens and farm, sounded attractive, however, and I decided to accept Dr. Paddon's invitation to visit him there. My log continues thus:

'Aug. 9th. At last I can tear myself away from Cartwright. These harbours are easy to get into, but everyone is so kind and hospitable that it is difficult to leave.

'9.30 A.M. Weighed with a fresh south-west wind and sailed across Huntingdon Flats according to Dr. L. Paddon's directions. The *Maraval*, drawing nine feet, habitually uses this channel, though the Sailing Directions state that there is no channel. I found two fathoms least water, though there may be less; suggest it be called *Emanuel* Channel.'

Off Entrance Island the wind dropped, and, seeing two boats fishing close by, I got out the cod jigger. This consists of two large hooks beneath a lead plate shaped like a fish three inches long. Within a few seconds of touching bottom I felt a tug and hauled up a fine cod of four or five pounds, and then another and another almost as quickly as I could haul them in. This seemed real fishing at last. But the breeze soon made again. Off Horse Chops Island I sighted the *Maraval*, and hailed her as she passed. She had developed shaft trouble and was bound to St. Anthony.

Passing Cape Porcupine I got on to Chart 375. This, the only one of this part of the coast, is on a scale of about one-tenth to a mile. It is only a very rough survey, many islets are not marked, and it is of no use for actual detail. Off George's Island I had to take in the kites in a hurry and reef down for a squall. Rain made it thick, and I hove to for a few minutes until it cleared. Then the wind went ahead and very light.

There were several anchorages inshore, but I felt shy of dodging about amid a maze of uncharted rocks and islands. There were several schooners, 'bankers,' ahead of me, and seeing one bring up, I ran astern of her and asked if I might hang on to her for the night. Accordingly they sent away a dory with a line and made me fast astern, so that I spent a very comfortable night. We were three or four miles from the land and in twenty-five fathoms, far too deep and exposed for me to lie to my own anchor. Her skipper came on board to see the yacht, and told me that the name of his ship was the *Corkum* of Grand Banks, Newfoundland.

These bankers are altogether larger and more able ships than the coastal fishing-schooners. Fishing in the open sea through the winter on the Newfoundland banks, they have to be really well found in rigging and sails. The local craft are not too well fitted out, with their sails patched and re-patched in a dozen places. At Sand Hill Cove I was aboard one ship ready to sail home with her catch. She was laden till her scuppers amidships were practically awash, and her deck was cluttered up with oil drums, boats, nets, &c., so that it was hardly possible to move. But with a thorough knowledge of the coast, harbours every few miles, and a powerful motor-boat to tow in a calm they are rarely caught out in bad weather, and casualties are very few.

The *Corkum* slipped me at 4.45 A.M. next morning, and with a light southerly air I reached past Saddle Island and then on to the narrows of Hamilton Inlet, but only making very slow progress against the current. The scenery here is very fine, with much higher hills, tree-clad on their lower slopes and softly grey above. The first reach is about two miles wide, and I got to the head of it close to Double Mer Point, where the channel divides between Double Mer and Lake Melville. The former is a narrow fiord thirty-five miles long, entirely unmapped. The wind had dropped, so I let go the dinghy's anchor with a light line to hold me against the current. A few minutes later I noticed a very ominous black cloud with curious spiral whorls approaching from ahead. Judging that there might be wind in it, I started to shorten sail, furled the jib, reefed the staysail, and put four rolls in the mainsail. I had just got into my oilskins when rain came down in a deluge, and it became almost dark—then the squall struck, just like a blow. What with the brilliant flashes of lightning, the terrific thunder-claps, howling of the wind, and the hissing roar of the rain, I felt bewildered. *Emanuel* started dragging rapidly to leeward (the dinghy's anchor is not much more than a toy), and

then lay over on her side like a dead thing. Water
came up on to the forecastle, where I was struggling to haul in the anchor line, higher than I have
ever seen it before. Although no headsail was set
and the anchor line was out on the weather bow,
she made no attempt to come up into the wind, but
just wallowed on her side. I was scared that she
might go right over, and jumped round to let fly
the peak halyards. Then she righted; up anchor,
staysail set, and off before it, running like an express train, though the rain was so heavy that I
could barely see the length of the ship; and it was
quite dark. I had the compass bearings of the
channel in my head, and knew the course on which
it was safe to run for a mile or two. I had noted
that when I saw the squall approaching, but I had
never met one like this before. It soon cleared so
that I could see the shores on each side, and the
wind abated to a moderate gale. Wet through as I
was, I did not feel inclined for several hours' beating to windward. To leeward lay Collingham Cove,
an anchorage which had been recommended me
and which I had noted on my way up four miles
inside the narrows. There was not much to show
from the chart where to anchor as I sailed in. I saw
a man ashore, shouted, and waved my hand towards the head of the cove. He understood at once,
roared out a quite indistinguishable reply, but
presently held up his hand, which I took to mean

a signal to round up. I obeyed, and, letting go, found myself in a well-sheltered anchorage.

The wind now settled for several days in the west, blowing fresh or strong, and I was able to make little progress. The narrows leading to Lake Melville continue for some twenty miles. I called at Rigolet, where there is another post of the Hudson Bay Company, and anchored in various little coves along the shore. Navigation was easy, since I had got into the area covered by the Canadian chart previously mentioned. In Moliak Cove I actually caught a trout. The yacht had been anchored off the mouth of a tiny stream, and on waking in the morning fish were to be seen rising all round. I put out an artificial minnow and presently pulled in a good-sized fish, which was promptly cooked for breakfast; but one really wants, of course, the company of an experienced fisherman. Once I got into Lake Melville, but had to put back on account of weather and nearly lost the dinghy, which I had foolishly left in tow instead of getting it on board.

On Henrietta Islands, near the western end of the narrows, there is a settlement of Eskimos, but when I sailed past the houses were deserted. Later I learned that they had gone a few miles down the coast to a wedding, at which one of their girls was being joined to a white man. The opinion seemed to be that she was a good worker, and that he was lucky to have got her. I had a few minutes' conversation with an Eskimo working for the Hudson Bay Company at Rigolet, and regretted very much not having the opportunity of seeing more of these engaging folk. They are much darker than I had expected, though not quite so black as a negro. The Labrador Eskimos have been in touch with white men for so long that they have adopted the clothes, houses, and food of their so-called superiors, though they retain their own language. They have been saved from extinction by the devotion of a small band of Moravian missionaries. They can mostly read and write, and are said to be very musical.

August 13th found me at anchor in Caravalla Cove at the entrance to Lake Melville, and my log continues: 'This is my 47th birthday; the review of the past years is not altogether satisfactory. It is perhaps as well that we do not always get our deserts in this world. I feel I am very fortunate in being able to make this cruise.'

It was still very squally from the west, and I delayed getting under way. I fitted new peak and throat halyards, and turned the jib and staysail halyards end for end. My running gear was lasting very well, and these were the first replacements since leaving England except for a jib-sheet. The halyards had had one season's use before I started. There would appear to be no necessity for using chain or wire running rigging in a small craft.

After lunch there was some improvement in the weather, and I got under way with four rolls in the mainsail, middle jib, and reefed staysail. Outside, in Lake Melville, the wind was unsteady, sometimes light and sometimes strong enough for the reefs to be needed. It was a long, tiresome plug to windward against a short choppy sea. Eventually I made Neveisik Island and looked into Pelter Cove, but the wind seemed blowing pretty well into the cove, and I did not care to go close in looking for the anchorage. Accordingly, and as it was getting late, I ran round under the lee of the island, and anchored in the open about a mile from the shore. The water shoals a long way off the shore.

The fresh westerly wind continued next day, and the prospect of reaching North-West River seemed remote. Abreast Neveisik Island on the southern shore of the mainland lay an inviting-looking sheltered bay named Port Disappointment. I sailed across to it with the idea of a ramble ashore. Climbing a neighbouring hill some 700 feet high, I had a most glorious view from the top. The wide expanse of Lake Melville with its islands lay below, while all around were spread mile after mile of dark, tree-covered expanse, above which the tops of hills showed their soft greys and browns.

My time for returning to St. John's was now getting rather short, and I reluctantly gave up the idea of reaching North-West River. Returning to the ship I hauled up the anchor, but while lifting it aboard I allowed, rather carelessly, the ship to forereach towards the head of the cove. Just as I put up the helm to bear away she grounded and remained fast. Both anchors were got out, but still she remained firm. Presently the wind veered to the north-east, blowing directly into the cove. A slight sea made, and *Emanuel* started to pound her keel on the sand. For a time I felt very anxious, but after some hours the tide rose and I got free, hauling out into deeper water. I had spent a very tiresome evening, and it was midnight before I had finished with the cables.

I made a quick run back next day to the narrows, but was held up off Snooks Cove by an adverse tide. I dropped anchor and went ashore, when I made the acquaintance of Mr. Baikie, a 'liviere' of the coast. He and his family made me very welcome, and insisted on providing me with a meal of most delicious smoked salmon. Their house was a substantial wooden shack with the usual huge wood-burning stove in the centre of the living-room. They also possess two more houses, one on Lake Melville as a half-way spring residence, and another for the winter at the head of Grand Lake, fifty miles inland. All through the winter they are quite alone except for the rare visit of an Indian or a white trapper. An aged grandmother lived with them, and accompanied them on their migrations. In spite of her years she was very bright, and enjoyed having her photograph taken.

When the tide turned I sailed on, and, after calling at Rigolet, anchored for the night in Mullins Cove. Here I met Mr. Austen Flower, a one-time guide to Sir Wilfred. There are, of course, no hotels or inns in Labrador, and the old-time idea of hospitality prevails. A passing stranger is asked in and offered refreshment as a matter of course.

Next morning after emerging from the narrows I kept close to the southern shore. During the afternoon the wind, a pleasant sailing breeze, came ahead. This time there was no friendly banker astern of which the yacht could be made fast for the night, and it was necessary to seek an anchorage among the fringe of uncharted islands off the coast. Presently I saw a schooner sailing close inshore behind the islands and the mast of another which appeared to be at anchor some miles to windward. After rounding several small islands which lay one-half or one-quarter of a mile apart, I saw an opening into the channel through which the schooner, now hidden behind the land, had sailed. I made this opening, and then was able to proceed with rather more confidence to the tiny sound where the other craft was at anchor. As there was not room to swing, I lay alongside her for the night.

I arrived safely back at Cartwright the following day, and was warmly welcomed at the Mission. Miss Hillier and Robbins arranged to come with me for a week-end sail, and we made a very pleasant excursion to Packs Harbour on the outer coast, where Miss Hillier was able to visit some former patients.

The wild berries, of which there is a great profusion everywhere in Labrador, were now becoming ripe, and we picked a dish of bakeapples to take back to the hospital. This is a yellow berry akin to a raspberry, but only growing a few inches high. It has a very distinctive flavour, and is palatable when stewed. In Newfoundland there is a small industry engaged in canning them. Blueberries and cranberries and several other sorts are abundant, while at Port Disappointment I had picked several pounds of red currants. These last were almost entirely without taste. A sort of wine can be made from some of these berries. This may well be the explanation of the Vinland of the Norsemen. Berries from which wine can be made might well be called grapes by northerners who had never seen real vines, although there is the admitted difficulty in that the Sagas tell of a German who was well acquainted with them. Helluland, which means land of flat stones, is particularly suggestive of the barren outer coast of Labrador.

I had supper at the Mission on my return, and

during the meal Miss Hillier complained of feeling unwell and retired. The picture of her in a black evening dress standing at the head of the table with her hand clasped to her breast remains very vividly in my memory. I saw her some months later in the hospital at St. Anthony looking just a ghost of her former bright self, and wasted almost to a skeleton. The bright colour of her cheeks and laboured breathing told their sinister tale, and just before I left Newfoundland I heard that she had died.

While I was at Cartwright H.M.S. *Scarborough* arrived with Mr. Ramsay MacDonald and his daughter on board. The ship only remained long enough to land a patient at the hospital.

I sailed from Cartwright on 20th August, bound south. A sore place on the back of my neck had been troubling me slightly for the last day or two, but it had not seemed of any importance. During the afternoon I felt considerable discomfort from it, and so brought up early in Hare Bay. There was no sign of any habitation anywhere around. The next day I felt really very seedy and in considerable pain. I felt altogether disinclined to continue sailing and lay all day in my bunk, occasionally applying hot boracic fomentations to my neck, which seemed to give some relief. I could neither eat nor sleep, and for the first time on the cruise felt really very lonely. I wondered if I was developing blood poisoning and in what stage of decomposition my body would be when it was found.

Next morning I felt rather better, though my neck was still very painful. There was a light northerly wind, fair for proceeding down the coast, but foul for returning to Cartwright, which, indeed, I was very loath to do. Off Gready Island, after sailing some ten miles, I saw a cloud of smoke and what appeared to be a whale being hauled up on a slip. With a number of men ashore there would be sure to be a medicine chest and help of sorts. I ran into the harbour and got quickly ashore, where I was greeted by Mr. Sullivan, the manager. He told me that the mail steamer *Kyle* was expected in an hour or so, and advised me to see her doctor; meanwhile I rested at their house. In due course the *Kyle* arrived. Her doctor advised me to go back to the hospital at Cartwright. This was a blow, as I had made no arrangements for leaving *Emanuel* and only had the clothes I stood up in. There was no time to return to the shore, but Mr. Lily of the whaling station offered to see about my ship. The passengers of the *Kyle* were very friendly, and as I came into the dining-saloon they stood up and drank my health. It was tantalising to see the generous spread of food which I felt much too ill to eat. It was a bad anti-climax coming back to Cartwright, but Dr. Kennard and the staff received me very kindly, and I was promptly put to bed with a hot poultice applied to my neck.

A couple of days after my return Dr. Kennard operated on my neck, which relieved the pain; next, an abscess developed in my thigh, which was cut open under a local anæsthetic. This was a curious sensation. I could feel my flesh being cut as if thick canvas was being sheared by a rather blunt knife, but there was no pain until the bottom of the incision was reached. Then there was a twinge, and the nurse had to more or less sit on my head for a moment. My temperature refused to go down, and a general infection of the body spread from the carbuncle on my neck. I suffered no particular pain, and did not feel especially ill as I lay in bed day after day wondering what was happening to my *Emanuel*. As week succeeded week I became more and more worried and impatient, and had visions of my ship being frozen in and perhaps crushed by the ice. Towards the end of September the Cartwright hospital closed down, and I was sent to St. Anthony on board the *Kyle*. It had got much colder, and ice formed in the puddles each night. A mysterious pain had developed in my left thigh and got progressively worse. For several nights I suffered considerable pain. X-rays showed nothing, but on diathermic treatment being given the pain slowly decreased.

After a fortnight at the hospital I was well enough to go to the inn, where I remained for another two weeks, gradually regaining my activity, although I remained somewhat lame for several weeks longer.

I owe a deep debt of gratitude to Dr. Curtis of St. Anthony and to Dr. Kennard and to all the staff of both hospitals.

On 16th October the Mission yacht *Strathcona* arrived with *Emanuel* in tow. It was a great thrill to see my ship again, but, of course, she was in a terrible state from damp, having been empty for two months. The weather had been very bad, with heavy gales from west and south-east, which had delayed the *Strathcona* for at least a week. *Emanuel* had shipped a good deal of water while in tow.

Blankets, bedding, &c., were dried out for me ashore and the ship's gear overhauled. The weather had turned bitterly cold, sleet and snow driving before a biting north-east wind. Three days later *Emanuel* was ready for sea, and I slipped from the Mission wharf in the presence of a large crowd of well-wishers who had come down to see me off. The morning was not too encouraging, with an occasional drizzle, but the fresh north-east wind was too good to waste. Running out under easy sail, I reached past the lighthouse and then set a course for Funk Island, 130 miles distant. It seemed quite strange to be sailing again after

two months on shore. After streaming the patent
log I found that the yacht was slipping along at
six knots, but it was bitterly cold in spite of all the
clothes I was wearing. These included a dicky,
which is a sort of blouse with a hood attached. It is
the usual winter wear on the coast, the hood and
sleeves being trimmed with fur. Mine was made of
a stout brown duck, but without the fur trimming.

The wind went light during the night, and most
of the following day was calm. During the afternoon my dead-reckoning put the yacht in the
vicinity of Snap Rock. There is rather an awkward
piece of navigation rounding Fogo Island. Funk
Island, lying thirty-two miles offshore, is an isolated rock one-third of a mile long, with several
outlying shoals which break. Half-way between
Funk Island and Fogo is Snap Rock, indicated
only by a cross on the chart, which presumably
meant less than six feet of water. My volume of
Sailing Directions had mysteriously disappeared
while down the Labrador coast, so that I was ignorant of the heights of Fogo and Funk Islands, and
consequently could not estimate the distance at
which they might be seen. During daylight there
would be no difficulty. I noticed on the bow a
disturbance in the water with a small cloud of
spray—evidently the looked-for Snap Rock; but
the disturbance seemed to be approaching and to
occur in several places: no rock, but a herd of

small whales. Presently heavy black clouds to windward accompanied by a falling glass made me take in the big staysail and prepare for a blow. As it turned out, my caution was unnecessary. At 4.45 P.M. I sighted a very distant speck of land bearing west-south-west. It had the appearance of a small island which could only be Funk, and in which case I was wildly out in my reckoning. More probably it was the tip of Fogo appearing above the horizon. The light died away before it was possible to fix my position, and I spent several most uncomfortable hours listening for possible breakers. During the early hours of the following morning the yacht lay without steerage-way, and I was able to get a couple of hours' sleep. The day broke fine and clear, but there was no wind and no land in sight. I felt fairly confident that Snap Rock was now behind me, and spent most of the day below reading or sleeping.

At 4.45 P.M. an air sprang up from the south-east, and a little later I sighted a schooner ahead, from which I deduced that I was not much out of my reckoning. The sun set in a bank of frightful lurid red clouds, and I longed for the safety of mid-Atlantic. It would have been most unpleasant to have been caught in a blow when near the land and uncertain of one's exact position. Again the signs of bad weather were not fulfilled. Before it got quite dark there was the suspicion of land on the bow, and as the ship was now sailing at a steady four knots, I hoped soon to find out where I was. At 8.25 P.M. a fixed white light was sighted, which should be the lighthouse on Cabot Island, and that distant rumble might be the surf; but I seemed to be raising the light with suspicious speed, and in a few minutes I realised that the noise was coming from a motor vessel. Obviously I must be on the right track. At 9 P.M. the real Cabot Island light was sighted. An hour later I sighted the dim outline of an islet a little on the starboard bow and not very far off. This should have been Gull Island, and it should have had a light on it, the absence of which added to the mystery of the night. However, with Cabot Island fairly close, there was now no doubt of my position. Subsequent working out of the previous courses and distances showed that I was eleven miles to the eastward of my reckoning. I was now, after two nights at sea, very sleepy. The wind had gone round ahead, so I put the yacht on the offshore tack and went below for a spell. I woke at 2.30 A.M., tacked, and found I could head up for Cabot Island, which was passed some four hours later. As I could now steer the course on the starboard tack, I decided to carry on for Cape Bonavista thirty miles away. Making a steady five knots through the smooth sea, the Cape was rounded at mid-day, and I then followed the grim and rocky eastern shore to Catalina. Some sunken rocks, on which the sea was breaking, lie off this part of the coast. There was something mysterious and alarming in the sight of a wave suddenly curling over and breaking in what appeared to be the open sea. I anchored in Catalina at 3.30 P.M., rather glad of a rest after three rather tiresome days during which I had made good 205 miles.

Next day there was a fresh north-east breeze, and I made a quick run to St. John's. The light went when I was some five miles from the port, but the entrance is lit, so that there was no difficulty in making it. A biggish swell was running, which broke heavily on the rocks. The wind did not blow home through the narrows, so that the yacht lost steerage way and gave me a few anxious moments. Breakers always look much nearer in the dark—and sound louder. In the swell *Emanuel* was unmanageable until I got out the sweep. I could then keep her heading in the right direction. Presently a draught of air pushed me through the narrows to the open water of the harbour where there was a working breeze which enabled me to reach the anchorage.

CHAPTER VII

A ROUGH PASSAGE

A VERY difficult problem now lay ahead. When I left England I had made no clear decisions beyond cruising on the Newfoundland and Labrador coast. The possible alternatives, now, were either to return to England, to cruise down the American coast, or to attempt the open sea passage to Bermuda and the West Indies. In any case, I had reckoned on getting away from Newfoundland before the summer was over.

Now the rapid approach of winter was imminent. At St. Anthony the weather had become comparable to an English winter at its worst, biting cold winds with snow and sleet and occasional frosts at night. There had been several heavy gales during my stay at the hospital, though I had been lucky in getting a quiet spell for the passage round to St. John's. Here the weather was much warmer, though the nights were getting cold. The reasonable course to take would have been to have laid up the yacht and returned home by steamer; but the expense of this with the double journey was too great for me to face. To follow the coast, with long nights coming on and the impossibility of reaching a warmer climate before mid-winter seemed hazardous in the extreme. Sometime or other I should surely have been caught in an onshore gale, or been wrecked in the attempt to make an unknown harbour in the dark. As a choice of evils the open sea passage of 1,100 miles to Bermuda was decided on.

That I was certain to meet some bad weather I knew very well, but I reckoned on soon getting into the warmer climate of the Gulf Stream, so that there would be no hardship from cold. The pilot chart showed prevailing winds to be north-west, before which *Emanuel* could run to the south. In the vicinity of Bermuda moderate winds, variable in direction, could be hoped for. It might be necessary to heave to for a day or two, but after that there should be a quiet spell during which sights could be obtained and the island reached without much difficulty.

The matter was naturally discussed with my friends at St. John's, and in opposing their suggestions that I should follow the coast I was wont to remark that once out in the open sea there were no tides or rocks; in fact, nothing to worry about except keeping the boat afloat. The last sentence instead of being a joke turned out to be a very grim reality, as the sequel will show.

Preparation for the passage occupied a few days. I ordered a new staysail, roped all round, and a middle-sized jib, both of really stout canvas. A chronometer watch was added to *Emanuel*'s equipment, and a full complement of spare ropes, food, and water taken on board. A chart of Bermuda had been ordered in ample time, but had gone astray in the post. I had visited the island during the War and remembered the main channel into the lagoon pretty well. There was a full description in my volume of Sailing Directions, and pilots were available. It seemed inadvisable to delay my departure for the several weeks necessary to obtain a new chart. None was to be procured in Newfoundland—nor could I purchase additional spare glasses for the cabin lamp.

Much hospitality was offered me by the residents of St. John's. Mr. Mauder showed me his partially completed model of *Emanuel*, which is to be placed in his collection. Mr. H. Alderdice made me a most generous present of rope from his factory, while his sister gave me a large joint of meat. Indeed, it almost seemed that my cruise was proceeding with official sanction, since Lady Anderson, the wife of the Governor, gave me a large plum cake.

By 3rd November *Emanuel* had been ready for sea for several days, but strong head winds had delayed my departure. The mysterious pain in the hip, a legacy of my recent illness, was gradually improving, though my normal activity had not quite returned, as was evidenced by my falling into the water while climbing on board from the wharf. The weather seemed on the mend, and the wind, though still strong, had veered to north of west, so that it would be possible to lay the course along the coast to Cape Race. After a morning of indecision I decided to start, and at 2 P.M. slipped from the wharf and hauled out to my anchor. I got under way with three and a half rolls in the mainsail and middle jib, not really enough sail, since *Emanuel* missed stays and fouled one of the schooners alongside the wharf. Her bowsprit caught against my mainsail, but luckily did not penetrate. One of her crew pushed me off, and I sailed away on the other tack, feeling rather foolish. *Emanuel*, like other small craft, does not handle too well without a staysail under adverse conditions. The wind, due to the surrounding hills, was blowing in strong gusts, succeeded by calms.

There was no time to hoist the reefed staysail, and I ran out of harbour through the narrows without further difficulty. An hour later Cape Spear was abeam. As I drew away from the land there were heavy squalls and a steep sea. *Emanuel* pounded ahead, making rather heavy weather of it and taking a good deal of water forward. The helm, as usual, was lashed, and I spent most of the time below.

Dusk fell early, and the jib was taken in; various shore lights showed up, and I could see that the yacht was making good progress. It got very cold, so I lit the stove at midnight. I was fairly wet and felt squeamish, but the wind seemed inclined to moderate, so that the motion became less violent. Cape Race was in sight at 2 A.M., after which I was able to doze for short periods. When day broke there was nothing in sight except the tumbling waves, and my ship seemed very small and lonely. All day long I sailed to the south-west, making about three-and-a-half knots. During the afternoon I set the jib, but the least exertion made me feel definitely sick. Those six weeks I had spent in bed had to some extent impaired my immunity. Most of the day and the following night I lay resting in the lee bunk.

November 5th. The wind had been gradually backing to the south of west, and by 1 A.M. I could not sail within a point of the course (S. 32 W. true). At daylight I reset the sails and stowed below the anchor. Again I felt almost exhausted after this very moderate exertion, and I suspect I was not too physically fit. It was a lovely, clear, sunny day and much warmer, but the sea was checking my progress, especially during the afternoon when the wind went light. I took the reef out of the staysail, hoping that the set of it had not been spoilt by reefing when new. Later the wind drew almost ahead, and I sailed on whichever tack was nearer my course. I remember thinking it was not a bad day as I sat smoking my pipe and watching the lovely sunset. All trace of seasickness had gone, and, the motion being more easy, I was able to cook an elaborate supper of lamb cutlets, peas, and potatoes. After clearing up I shortened sail for the night and lay down to sleep. A ship's lights were seen passing several miles away; it was the only vessel sighted on this voyage.

November 6th. I awoke at 1.30 A.M. and had a look round. There was no change in the ship, and she was holding her course to the west. At noon I had only made good fifty-two miles in the preceding twenty-four hours, but later my progress improved, sailing four to five knots pretty well on the course. After dark there was a fairly good reception on my wireless set, and I was able to identify several American stations. The motion had become too violent for cooking, but I could boil a kettle and supped off Bovril and Shredded Wheat. The latter goes very well with tinned cream. The weather had become so warm that for most of the day I only wore one jersey.

During the night the wind gradually increased, and at daylight was blowing a moderate gale. The jib had to come in, and more rolls in the mainsail were needed. Then, pulling the staysail to windward, I hove-to. It was very wet working on the forecastle, and I went below feeling pretty miserable, but thankful the weather was warm. The lanyard of the topmast stay had chafed through, so I had to haul the jib halyards out to the end of the bowsprit as a preventer. The dinghy had shifted, but I was able to get her back in the chocks, and passed an extra lashing round her. I also got the sea-anchor ready. This is a large canvas bag or drogue which, by its drag in the water, is supposed to keep a boat's head to the sea in rough weather.

By noon the glass had fallen to 29.40, and the wind was blowing a full gale with a heavy breaking sea. It seemed time for the sea-anchor. I got up the anchor chain and shackled it on to the drogue. *Emanuel* has a standing chain bobstay which would be certain to chafe through any hemp hawser. Then down staysail, and overboard with the sea-anchor. The chain took charge, and almost the whole thirty fathoms ran out before I could pass a stopper round it. The motion was far too violent to keep one's feet on the forecastle; the work had to be done kneeling or lying, with heavy splashes washing over one's body. One badly wants a third hand, but teeth again came in useful for holding ropes' ends. Then the mainsail was got down. This was an awkward job, as *Emanuel* was now lying well off the wind and the gaff sagged away to leeward. After a sharp tussle I got the sail secured with the boom lashed to the gunwale. Then back into the cockpit to see how she lay and what sort of weather she was making of it. This was

Emanuel's first experience of lying to a sea-anchor. It was not too good. She lay in the trough of the sea, broadside on, and heavy breaking seas continually broke over the cockpit, all the water finding its way into the bilge. The cabin floor was well awash and pumping an immediate necessity. 'Nothing to worry about except to keep the ship afloat.' The water swishing about in the bottom was finding a lot of unexpected grit, pieces of sodden paper and other oddments which continually choked the pump, necessitating undoing the nuts and taking it apart several times. One sea broke into the cockpit with such violence that the steering compass and cabin steps were thrown into the cabin. It seemed very doubtful whether I should be able to keep her afloat, but the need for action, if only pumping, kept me from feeling too frightened. Some half-hour's work freed the ship.

At 3 P.M. the glass started to rise and the wind lulled. I got up the new jib as a riding sail, tack to the counter, head to the peak halyards, and the clew secured forward. This kept the yacht's head to the sea, and she rode the waves very well, but every now and then the jib flapped so viciously that it seemed something must carry away; however, everything held. The wind and sea gradually took off, and I spent an easy night.

Next morning the wind was light. At daylight

I got in the sea-anchor. It was heavy work at first with thirty fathoms of chain hanging over the bows, but later the chain came in with suspicious ease. The iron ring of the sea-anchor had torn away, so that the bag had collapsed. I set jib and staysail and left the riding sail up so that *Emanuel* sailed herself to the west, with the wind a little before the beam. All the morning was occupied by making a spreader for the sea-anchor out of the boom crutches which I cut up for the purpose. Even this very simple carpentry was difficult and laborious owing to the violent motion.

During the afternoon I set the mainsail, which had the effect of steadying the yacht, but with the head-wind the progress was slight.

The fresh meat had all gone bad owing to the warm weather, so for supper I opened one of the Newfoundland delicacies, tinned 'Turs.' This is a kind of sea-bird—not at all bad. My log notes 'First meal in comfort,' but this was an exaggeration in view of a previous supper already noted. I heard my first time-signal this night, Daventry, very faint but distinct. Just before midnight I woke rather bewildered to find the wind had shifted to north-west. I trimmed the sails and went to sleep again.

The ship made good progress during the night, but next morning at daybreak it was flat calm and we rolled viciously. I lowered all sails to prevent chafe. After breakfast I fitted lashings and hooks so as to spread the dinghy's sail over the cockpit in hopes of keeping out some of the water during the next gale. I also refitted the topmast stay lanyard. Coming aft, I slipped overboard. I kept hold of the gunwale and pulled myself aboard again. There was no real danger, as the yacht had no way on.

At 3.30 P.M. I made sail to a light south-east air which gradually increased, so that by 8 P.M. *Emanuel* was again close-reefed, and for the most of the night hove-to. A violent thunderstorm passed overhead, during which I secured a coil of copper wire to the rigging, leaving the end to trail overboard.

November 10th. At daylight the wind had eased sufficiently to let draw and proceed on my course. From noon onwards it was pleasant sailing weather almost for the first time since St. John's. The water felt quite warm to the touch. During the evening the last of my lamp chimneys broke, leaving only a stump. The lamp could be used turned low, and giving a very dim light. This made the early hours of darkness rather intolerable. For supper I could supplement with a candle, but there were not enough of these to burn continuously.

November 11th. Wind was light from 2.30 A.M. and came east, moderate at daylight. For a few hours I sailed with full mainsail, but at 10.45 it was necessary to reef. It was actually too warm to wear a jersey and pleasant to go barefooted. I got sights this day, and found I was within nine miles of the dead-reckoning. The wind gradually increased, and at dusk *Emanuel* was close-reefed.

During the early hours of the night she pounded, spray-swept, through the darkness. Heavy seas broke on board forward, and a good deal of water found its way aft. I had fitted a new strainer to the pump suction, which gave no further trouble.

I was loath to heave to when making good progress, but soon after midnight it was blowing with gale force, and the ship was labouring so heavily that I was forced to do so. Daylight revealed minor casualties. The staysail tack lashing had chafed through and had to be replaced. The spinnaker boom topping-lift had carried away, but the bracket aloft kept the boom in place. There was a big sea running, and occasionally a crest broke against the side with a loud crash. At 9 A.M. I got out the sea-anchor and set the storm-jib as a riding sail, but this is not big enough to keep *Emanuel* head to sea. However, there seemed no immediate danger of foundering.

Meals had been difficult. For breakfast I would usually make porridge from 'Three-minute Oat Flakes,' which could be eaten direct from the saucepan. The motion had generally been too bad for frying eggs and bacon. The latter had started

getting mouldy after a day or two, so I had cooked
all of it, and had been eating the slices cold. Early
in the voyage I had opened a bottle of boiled cod
fish, and in order to utilise it before it went bad had
eaten it at each meal for three days. Bread went
mouldy after two or three days, but this was no
hardship as my ship's biscuits were quite appetising. I had taken a good supply of brazil nuts,
which went well with dates or raisins.

3 P.M. Wind was south-west, and *Emanuel* was
drifting away from her port. To lessen this I
improvised a second sea-anchor out of the old staysail, which I secured with a bridle to my large
warp. One corner was weighted with the dinghy's
anchor. I doubt whether it was very efficient. Next
morning found *Emanuel* still afloat after another
tempestuous night. No sleep had been possible, as
it had been necessary to pump for ten to twenty
minutes each hour. The sail over the cockpit did
not seem much good, but with daylight the weather
moderated. After fortifying myself with breakfast
I hauled in the sea-anchors. The staysail had gone
adrift completely, and the drogue had burst beyond repair; so that was that. I made sail and tried
to proceed, but it was too rough, and I had to
heave to until the evening.

November 14th. At 4 A.M. the jib-sheet, rove
new at St. John's, parted. The sail was got down
without damage. Fresh head-winds persisted, but

nothing in the way of incident occurred until just before midnight, when the roller-reefing gear failed. The socket in the boom had worn so that it unrolled. Luckily the wind was no more than fresh at the time. My rough log notes briefly, 'Set trysail,' but this represents several hours of arduous work. The first operation was getting the mainsail down, a difficult job single-handed in the dark with the whole sail unrolled. Next it had to be unbent, and the mass of heavy sodden canvas dragged into the cabin. I needed a rest after this, and made some coffee. Then I lugged the trysail from the spare bunk of the fore cabin, secured it to the gaff and boom and finally hoisted it.

November 15th. Wind continued all day from the south or south-west, gradually freshening with a falling glass. Obviously another gale was approaching. I felt utterly discouraged and in no mind to meet it. Completely worn out by the continual rough sea, the slightest exertion seemed a tremendous effort. Even to boil a kettle seemed too much trouble, and I lay in the lee bunk reading cheap magazines. At dusk it was again blowing so hard that I had to heave to. It was a frightful night, literally full of fright, as I listened to the seas crashing against the cabin's sides. Every timber shuddered, and it seemed impossible that the hull could stand up to such hammering. Once a specially heavy sea broke fairly on the beam.

The yacht was thrown right on her side and flung
bodily to leeward. Odds and ends were thrown out
of the weather rack in the cabin and a note-book
lodged against the ceiling on the lee side. I thought
of Voss returning to port with the mark of his stove
on the cabin roof. Cushions, a spare battery, and
other gear were hurled into the water washing
about on the cabin floor. About 3 A.M., when the
glass had fallen to 28.90, I heard the slatting of a
sail. I jumped to the cabin hatch just in time to see
the trysail split across horizontally. Part flew aloft,
tore the gaff from the mast and wrapped itself round
the cross-trees, streaming out to leeward like a
huge banner. The other part of the sail gave one
vicious flap, snapped the main boom like a carrot,
and collapsed overboard. At the same time I noticed that the dinghy had gone, taking with it the
lee runner. The wind seemed to be blowing with
hurricane force, and I thought the flapping canvas
aloft must pull the mast out of her. It was difficult
to know what to do—if anything could be done.
After a few moments' thought I decided to get the
staysail down and let the yacht drift. Crawling over
the reeling deck, I forced my way forward through
the blinding, stinging spray and hauled down the
sail. The forecastle was like a half-tide rock, and I
had to cling on for dear life to avoid being swept
overboard. Extra lashings were put on the staysail,
and the simple job of stowing this sail took some

time, perhaps half an hour. I had not waited to put on an oilskin, though, indeed, a bathing dress would have been the only suitable rig; but the water was comparatively warm.

Getting back to the cabin I found three or four inches of water on the cabin floor. So this was really the end; I thought of the yacht's jesting motto, 'England is an overcrowded country any-way.' It seemed to be coming true, but I did not feel like laughing. I pictured the water rising in the cabin, *Emanuel*'s last plunge, and those few awful moments choking in the black water. But after all, many thousands of better men have been drowned before me, and I may as well make an effort. I started the pump; for a quarter of an hour it was doubtful if I was gaining on the water, and every now and then a fresh splash would wash over the cockpit; but after forty-five minutes' work the ship was free and my hopes rose. At daylight the two stern hawsers were put out and some three feet of the staysail was hoisted. I packed the cockpit with the remains of the trysail, which I had hauled on board (half the broken boom had gone), to-gether with several other spare sails. Thus there was not so much room for the water when a wave slopped over the counter. *Emanuel* then lay rather better. I have never seen such a sea before, huge rolling mountains with great valleys between, while every now and then the cross swells would cause a pyramid of water to rise up with almost vertical sides. *Emanuel* was flung about like a cork, swinging broadside on when a steep sea caught her stern. But here is a point of interest which might be emphasised. Unless she was actually caught by the breaking crest it seemed not to matter which way she lay, nor actually how steep was the face of the overtaking waves. She lifted buoyantly to them all. Poor little yacht, what a wreck she looked. The remains of the trysail had blown away, but the gaff was dangling aloft and the halyards and stays had wrapt round each other in dreadful confusion. The beading round the cabin top had been broken and the canvas covering torn away. And alas for the dinghy! There was nothing to be done. The sea looked so terrifying that I could not bear to look at it, and I remained below all day.

The day passed slowly, and I dreaded the dark hours. During the night the wind veered to north and north-west, and gradually took off. Next morning, 17th November, it had gone light, leaving a huge swell in which *Emanuel* rolled helplessly. It seemed urgent to clear up the wreckage aloft. I was able to get the gaff on deck and free the peak halyards, to which I fixed the boatswain's chair. I secured myself to the mast with one of the mainsail ties, and then, with an effort and some bruising, hauled myself up to the cross-trees, so that I was able to clear the throat halyards. After getting in the stern

lines I hoisted the big staysail abaft the mast,
sailing to the south-west. Later in the day this
was replaced by the mainsail, set close-reefed
without a boom, but the wind dropped completely.

November 18th. Light airs or calms all day.
For the last few days my rough log contained but
few entries. Reaching port seemed improbable, so
that I had no heart to write it up. I was now about
500 miles from Bermuda and seriously crippled.
With the continual rough sea it seemed unlikely
that sights would be obtained, without which I
should never find the island even if I succeeded in
reaching its vicinity. The prevailing wind was
westerly, and I anticipated being blown helplessly about the Atlantic until food and water
gave out in about two months' time. More than
ever did I feel depressed after working out a sight
which put me ninety miles west of the reckoning. I
seriously contemplated running for the Azores.
Having lost the trysail, I could not heave to in the
next gale and risk my mainsail blowing away. It
was fitted with a row of eyelets for reefing, but
the reef cringle on the leach was not tabled very
heavily. Already I had been economising on my
water, and had been thinking of how I might
catch rain in a sail, though only in a calm would
this be feasible. My chronometer watch had been
going very irregularly, but having picked up two

American stations which gave the time, this did not matter.

By the forenoon the swell had gone down considerably, so that I was able to get aloft to the top of the mast and clear the remaining ropes. I wanted the topsail halyards so that this sail could be set over the reefed mainsail. The calm continued for the next two days, weather being bright and sunny, so that most of the cabin gear could be dried. My shore-going trousers had been hanging in a wardrobe flooded with the bilge water. One morning I actually bathed, but the prolonged inactivity was trying.

November 21st. For six days I had made no progress toward my port, but this morning just before dawn a light air made from the north-north-west. I made sail, hoisting the topsail over the mainsail, which could only be set close-reefed without the boom. Pleasant conditions did not last long. At 7 A.M. it was blowing hard from the east, and the after canvas had to come in. I felt the lack of a companion; with another hand to take his turn at the helm the mainsail might have been kept on her, driving the yacht hard. Alone, with all the work of the ship, preparing food, &c., one has neither time nor mental energy to sit at the tiller for long periods. However, *Emanuel* ran very well under the jib and staysail, making four and a half or five knots. The direction of the wind had decided my course of action, to run for Bermuda. It was an uncomfortable night, wind and sea increasing, though the glass remained steady at 30.20. Again daylight showed minor casualties. The forestay lanyard had chafed through and also the bolt rope on the luff of the staysail, the sail itself being rather badly torn. But the damage was below the reef cringle, so that the sail could be set reefed. At 10 a.m. the sea was becoming menacing, and I put out the stern hawsers. The patent log, of course, had to come in, so that the distance run could only be guessed at.

The following W.T.'s signal was made this day from Captain Blagrove of H.M.S. *Norfolk* to the Admiral at Bermuda. 'At 11.50, in position 35.49 N. 59.28 W., passed small craft, cutter rig, under foresail only. Name of craft and destination unknown. Apparently all well with her.' I never saw the *Norfolk*, but the position agrees closely with mine. I am glad now that Captain Blagrove did not attempt communication, as I might have made distress signals and abandoned the yacht. I am glad I did not have to make the decision. This message was published in the Bermuda Press. It was there blowing a gale under the influence of a hurricane 100 miles to the southward. The usual course for a hurricane is north-east, right over my track, and it was not expected that the yacht would survive. In actual fact, the hurricane was deflected to the south by the belt of high pressure through which *Emanuel* was sailing. It then described a complete circle and dispersed. It is quite unusual for a hurricane to occur at this time of the year.

November 23rd. Wind moderated during the morning, and stern lines were hauled in. At noon Bermuda should have been 280 miles, reckoning my speed for the previous twenty-four hours at three knots. I got a very rough sight for latitude. A sextant unfortunately needs two hands. The only place where it is possible to keep one's feet without hand support is on the cabin steps, bracing one's body against the companionway. When a splash seems likely the sextant is held under one's oilskin. Then as the ship rises to the top of the wave an attempt is made to snap the sun touching the horizon.

There was not much change in the weather conditions during the next day, except that the wind was gradually drawing round to the east and north-east. I had been making good progress, with twenty-four-hour runs of 105 and 108 miles, good going under headsails only. Noon of the 25th found me by reckoning about 100 miles north-east of Bermuda. I got a very rough latitude, but my longitude depended on the courses and distance sailed during the last five days. Actually it must have been 100 miles in error. I decided to sail due south to the parallel of Bermuda and then steer west true. This would give me the best chance of finding the island, though, discouraged as I was, it seemed a slender one. There was too much wind for the mainsail, so I hoisted a jib abaft the mast. It set badly, but with the staysail forward *Emanuel* kept a fair course with the wind abeam, forging ahead at about two knots.

By 9.30 P.M. the wind had increased to gale force, and I had to run before it steering west-north-west. This was the direction *Emanuel* seemed to take most easily, and I was past caring and too tired to make much effort to keep her nearer the proper course. Bermuda lay somewhere ahead, and I might—or might not—sight it. I wondered what to do if I did not sight it. The American coast was some 500 miles beyond; I had no charts, but had once been into Chesapeake Bay. With luck there was a chance of blundering in there; or I might try to work 1,000 miles to the south and find one of the West India islands. Both prospects were pretty bleak.

I got some sleep during the night. At 3.30 A.M. I woke to find the yacht steering south-west by south. Day broke slowly with an overcast sky and occasional drizzle, still blowing hard from east-north-east. Somewhere about 7 A.M., not long after full daylight, I noticed the colour of the water looked queer—a lighter and rather sickly blue. Surely it could not be shallow water! But quite de-

finitely it looked different from the previous day.
Anyway I thought I had better look round the
horizon, and to my amazement I saw distant, low-
lying land ahead. It was incredible, but there was
no doubt as to the reality of that dark ridge that
showed against the horizon each time the yacht
lifted to the top of a wave. But what about the reef?
With land on that bearing, I must be sailing right
on to it. As if in answer, a small beacon showed up
on the starboard bow a quarter of a mile away and
directly to leeward. There was not much time. I
tore loose the lashings on the mainsail and made a
desperate effort to hoist it. All went well, and with
aftersail set *Emanuel* was soon under control. I
hove to, heading north, to consider the situation.
Now was felt the absence of a chart. A recent
correction to the Sailing Directions stated that the
beacon on the North Rock had been destroyed.
Very likely it had been rebuilt since, and there was
a rock alongside it which sometimes showed above
water. I assumed, correctly as it turned out, that
it was the North Rock that I saw. Close-hauled on
the port tack I headed east-south-east, and for a
while I steered this course in the hope of weather-
ing the eastern edge of the reef and entering by the
ship channel. Soon, however, breakers showed up
fine on the weather bow, and it was clear that a
dead beat to windward lay ahead of me.

A heavy sea was running, and *Emanuel* had all

the sail she needed, with reefed staysail and mainsail. She was manageable and would stay with
care, but the bearing of the beacon changed very
slowly. After an hour or so it was evident that I
was not gaining much to windward. The Sailing
Directions stated that there was a passage on
either side of the North Rock. Without chart or
local knowledge it seemed a desperate chance, but
for a time I seriously considered attempting one of
the passages, and hoping that the breakers would
guide me. In an hour's time I should have finished
with this long-endured knocking about—in safety
or otherwise. I was so worn out that I was almost
callous as to which it should be, but it seemed as if
there was a duty to my ship: not to wreck her after
she had brought me so far and endured so much.
I was doing no good trying to work to windward
and put up the helm with the idea of running round
the reef to leeward of the island. There should be
smooth water there; anything to get away from
this endless tossing.

Emanuel tore through the water, surging forward as each wave carried her along. My only
guides as to the course were the breakers on the
reef. These were by no means easy to distinguish
from the breaking crests all round. There was no
definite line of surf, but only isolated patches where
the waves appeared to break with greater violence
than elsewhere. Presently Ireland Island showed

up, and also the dockyard buildings; I gradually worked round to the south-west and the south. The reef here extends five miles off the shore.

As the land drew to the northward it provided shelter from the sea, which went smooth quite suddenly—suspiciously so. The water was a very light blue, and what was the meaning of those dark patches? No doubt whatever as the keel grated over the coral. I had sailed over the reef. Was *Emanuel* to be wrecked after all? I could see the houses on the shore, but I had no dinghy, and it was too far to swim. I was then steering south-east with the wind abeam. Putting the helm up, I sailed towards the south to the open sea, dodging the dark patches as best I could. The keel touched slightly once more, but slid clear, and it was soon apparent that I was in deeper water and clear of the patches. A long tedious beat to windward along the southern shore was now in prospect. There would not be as much shelter as I had hoped, as it was evident that after rounding Gibb's Hill, the wind would be pretty well along the shore. The only practicable harbour lay at least ten miles to windward, and there was no hope of making it before dark.

The short, steep waves drenched the cockpit with stinging spray, making it almost more uncomfortable than when in the bigger ones of the open water. I lashed the helm and retired to the cabin to get some food. It was then about 1 P.M., and I had not had any time for breakfast. Suddenly the blast of a motor-horn sounded above the thudding of the spray. Rushing on deck, I saw a large motor-boat close to the yacht. Wildly I waved a rope's end, tingling all over with excitement and relief. I had won after all. After some manœuvring a line was secured which promptly broke. I then got out a stout grass line, and was soon in tow once more. For some time we barely made headway against the wind, but very slowly the land drew nearer, so that we were more sheltered. Now making better progress, the motor-boat pulled *Emanuel* through a maze of coral patches, and at last reached a small land-locked bay called Ely's Harbour. Here, about 3.30 P.M., I dropped anchor, in safety at last.

BERMUDA

CHAPTER VIII

BERMUDA

I FOUND myself in a small land-locked bay. To seaward several small islets protected the mouth, leaving only the very narrow channel through which we had entered. The reef extends some miles from the shore, and is studded with coral heads within a few feet of the surface. In places the channel between these is only a few yards wide, and even with the help of the occasional beacons it would have been quite impracticable without adequate local knowledge. The shores, rising gently to 150 feet, were covered with tall cedars, amongst which were dotted the gleaming white cottages of the inhabitants. Here and there lay beaches of white coral sand against which the wavelets lapped gently. The brilliantly hued water was so clear that I could see the anchor on the bottom.

'Port after storm' indeed, and an amazing contrast to my situation of a few hours earlier. It was a strange feeling, almost of coming to life again after days when I had not really expected to come through. It was an overwhelming satisfaction to know that my ship and I had won, to say nothing of the relief from days and nights of sheer physical

175

terror. However philosophic one may be about one's cosmic importance, the immediate prospect of struggling in the water is distinctly unpleasant, especially when for hours and hours there is nothing else to do except think about it.

The motor-boat which had towed me in was manned by a Portuguese fisherman and a coloured crew. They came on board and stowed my sails. Before this was completed Dr. Sweeney, the port medical officer, came alongside in his launch. He waived all formalities about granting pratique, and straight away asked me up to his house. He told me not to bother about changing, so I hurriedly thrust some dry clothes into a bag and accompanied him. After a few minutes' drive we arrived at his house, and he ushered me into the drawing-room, where a tea-party was in progress.

Bareheaded, barefooted, dressed in an old blue jersey and ragged serge trousers which had been cut down into shorts, and with three weeks' growth of beard, I must have looked a strange object, and I wish I could have heard the guests' subsequent description of the extraordinary apparition which confronted them. But I was far past caring for social etiquette. Dr. Sweeney and Mrs. Sweeney were extremely kind, and after a good meal, a bath, and dry clothes I felt much refreshed. I stayed with them for about a week, and Dr. Sweeney is of opinion that this rest prevented a possible breakdown on my part. Though I was a stone and a half under my normal weight, owing partly to my illness and partly to the difficulty and labour of cooking proper meals during the voyage, I felt fitter, physically, than I had when I left St. John's. The pain in my hip had disappeared.

The next few days were fine, although the hurricane warning remained in force, windows and doors being boarded up with special shutters. I was able to get the cabin and gear dried out; the cushions on the bunks, of course, were soaked, but most of the blankets had kept fairly dry in the fore cabin. In the meantime I arranged for the dockyard to undertake the necessary repairs, and in a few days' time had *Emanuel* towed round there.

The dockyard happened to be particularly busy, and *Emanuel* had to lie there for about two months. I found myself an honorary member of the wardrooms of the various ships, and the captain of the dockyard very kindly put me up at his house for three weeks, so that the time passed pleasantly enough, although at times I felt rather impatient at the prolonged inactivity. Assistance in refitting my rigging was provided by several of the ships. I found two old shipmates who had married and settled in the island.

The Bermudas consist of a string of narrow islands arranged roughly as a crescent twenty miles long, with a greatest width of about one mile. To the north and west the coral reef extends up to nine miles, leaving a considerable expanse of deep water between it and the land. The nearest mainland is the American continent, 500 miles distant, while the West Indies are nearly 1,000 miles to the south.

Neither the date nor the circumstances of their discovery is known, but it must have been very soon after Columbus, since sailing-ships coming home from the West Indies would be forced to stand to the northward out of the trade-wind belt, and would ordinarily pass close to Bermuda. They were colonised by the English in 1612. At present the population is about 29,000, rather more than half being the coloured descendants of the slaves imported by the early settlers.

The general appearance of the scenery is given by the indigenous cedars (really juniper), but much of the ground is cultivated with onions, strawberries, and other vegetables, and there are numerous banana plantations. Papaws, Royal Palms, and Palmettos are common in the gardens. As a whole, the islands have rather a suburban aspect, especially round Hamilton, although along the south shore there are some very lovely wild bits. The sea is usually of a brilliant colour, with varying shades of brown, blue, and green according to the depth and nature of the bottom.

The most important industry is catering for

American and Canadian visitors. This industry was given a great impetus by prohibition in the U.S.A., and the habit seems continuing. Motor-cars are not allowed, bicycles for the poor and carriages for the rich being the mode of conveyance, besides the railway, which runs from end to end of the islands. Certainly the roads are not fit for cars, but it used to be said that with a car one could explore the whole of the islands in a day. By horse carriage it takes several days, so that visitors are retained for a longer period.

The gardens attached to the larger houses are very striking. All the usual temperate flowers do well, and, in addition, there is the foliage effect of palms and other tropical plants. Before I left the oleanders were just coming out, but I missed their full glory.

The climate is just cool enough in winter for an evening fire to be a luxury but not a necessity. There is a great deal of wind and rain, although between times there are lovely bright, sunny days. In April it was like a fine English June, and the sea-water was warm enough to make bathing pleasant.

Rather more than half the population are negroes. There seems to be no Colour question, both races having full political rights; but the franchise has a property qualification which in effect insures that the Government is in the hands of the whites. The coloured folk form the working class of the population; wages and the standard of living are high, and the people appear, superficially at any rate, to be very contented. There is no social intercourse between the two races, but all the Bermudans that I met spoke well of the coloured people, and remarked that they were mostly a very decent lot. Another element in the population is formed by the Portuguese immigrants from the Azores. They are a steady, hard-working people, and most of the market gardening is in their hands. The African temperament does not seem to take kindly to the long hours and steady work which the land demands, and the negro is better employed as a fisherman, coachman, servant, or shop-keeper, where the effort is more intermittent. If this is really so, the old plantation slavery must have been even more cruel than one supposed. Such of the coloured people as I happened to meet were civil and friendly.

An echo of an ancient controversy still persists in Bermuda. Women do not have the vote, but are agitating for it, without, apparently, much success. Really, one thought that was a controversy settled quite a long time ago, but I suspect that the opposition comes from the feeling that if any alteration were made in the suffrage, far-reaching reforms might be demanded by the less well-to-do section of the population. For instance, there is a tax on cycles, but not on carriages.

During my enforced idleness in the dockyard, I had plenty of time to form plans for the future. Of one thing I was quite certain, and that was no more ocean passages until the winter was over. My original idea had been to call at Bermuda for only a few days and then continue down to the West Indies, where I should cruise for the winter, with the possibility of the Panama Canal and home across the Pacific. I made some tentative inquiries as to the feasibility of shipping *Emanuel* home on board a steamer, but finally decided to remain at Bermuda until April, and then sail home *via* the Azores.

Christmas came, and I enjoyed the unusual experience of two Christmas dinners, an early one at the house of Commander Morrell, my old shipmate, and a later one with Lieut.-Commander and Mrs. Bury of the dockyard.

In the early part of February *Emanuel* was ready for sea again. A new main boom had been made and a defective chain-plate replaced. New canvas had been fitted over the cabin, and the yacht had been hauled up and painted. An old boat-builder living in Somerset Island had made me a nine-foot, flat-bottomed punt to replace the lost dinghy. I was at last free to sail about the islands, and for the next two months had the pleasantest time imaginable. My headquarters were in Cavello Bay, Somerset, Riddells Bay, or in one of the many anchorages around Hamilton. I had made many acquaintances, and on most days had friends out sailing with me. I made several trips to St. George's at the eastern end of the islands, on one of which I met Commander Moorhead of the meteorological station. He showed me the weather maps of the North Atlantic for the period of my last voyage, and it was interesting to note that he had postulated a small and deep disturbance close to the position of my worst storm. On one occasion I picked up a mooring off Hinson Island, and made the acquaintance of Major and Mrs. Kitchener, who reside there. Acquaintance ripened into friendship, and finally resulted in Major Kitchener offering to sail back to England with me. I am particularly indebted to Mrs. Kitchener for agreeing to her husband going off on what her parents considered a wild and perilous expedition.

I decided to sail on 16th April, as by that time the gale frequency would be very much reduced. A few days before my departure I arranged to give an 'At Home' to all the people whose hospitality I had enjoyed. Accordingly, I arranged with the Inverurie Hotel to provide tea, and sent out invitations to some eighty guests. When the day came I put *Emanuel* alongside the hotel jetty so that my friends could see over her. Unfortunately it poured with rain, and only half the promised guests arrived. I was honoured, however, to receive Lady Cubitt, the wife of the Governor, and Admiral Sir Matthew Best, the Commander-in-Chief.

The weather continued very unsettled, and I decided to postpone my departure for a week.

With two of us on board the fresh-water supply needed augmenting. This was done by embarking nine four-and-a-half gallon kerosene tins. Five of these were stowed under the cockpit and four on the cabin floor. We were the recipients of presents too numerous to mention, but a gallon of rum from one of the men-of-war and four dozen bottles of beer from a Canadian friend were especially appreciated. Other gifts included cakes, chocolates, tinned fruits, and meats; and finally two bunches of bananas, which latter were hung up in the rigging. By the time all was stowed away *Emanuel* was some inches below her usual draught.

I made a canvas lining for the cockpit with a hole in it over the drain-pipe. This should make the after part of the ship effectively water-tight; but it was never necessary to use it.

For some time previously my teeth had been giving trouble, and on visiting a dentist it was found necessary to extract three of them. This subsequently made it rather difficult to eat ship's biscuit.

CHAPTER IX

HOMEWARD BOUND

BY 23rd April the weather had been quiet for several days, and at 2.30 P.M., all adieus having been said, we shoved off from the Hinson Island jetty. Mr. Bluck, Kitchener's father-in-law, took us in tow with his motor-boat, and we proceeded out into the sound. We had a very fine send-off, several other motor-boats accompanying us, from which our friends cheered and waved. After rounding Hogfish Beacon we made sail to a light head-wind, and started to beat through the main channel. It was soon apparent that we could not get clear of the islands before dark, so we ran into Bailey's Bay for the night—and realised that the spare batteries for the wireless set had been left behind. This was the first time that I had forgotten anything, but we were able to telephone for them to be sent on by an early train.

Next morning on going ashore to meet the train we encountered Mrs. Kitchener and her daughter Betty. They had heard about the forgotten batteries and had come down with them for a last good-bye. The wind was still light, north-easterly, blowing directly into the entrance.

As this was very narrow, we got a local motor-boat to tow us out, and then, making sail, we stood seaward. Mrs. Kitchener and Betty climbed down to the rocks at the entrance, and waved. Gradually we drew away, and their two figures diminished to two little dots, and finally became indiscernible from the rocks. Topsail set, Lee-O, and we could fetch St. Catherine's Point at the north-east extremity of the islands; then through the buoys marking the narrows, round the Fairway Buoy, and *Emanuel*, after her five months' rest, was at sea again.

A big cruise ship lay at anchor just ahead, and we sailed close under her stern, while her passengers looked down from the towering deck above. I wonder how many of them would have wished to change ships had they known whither we were bound.

At 12.15 P.M. departure was taken from the Fairway Buoy, north-west a quarter of a mile, and the patent log streamed. *Emanuel* was steadied on her course, east by south, with the wind just before the port beam. The wind was light and the sea smooth, and *Emanuel* glided over the easy swell, gently rising and falling with hardly a roll, making four knots; 1,800 miles of open ocean lay before us.

It was with very real regret that I watched Bermuda dwindle astern, thinking of all the pleasant friends that I had made there, few of whom was it likely that I should see again. But my home lay ahead. Kitchener did not say what he thought.

I should like to put here on record my debt to my crew. Although used to boats he had little experience in yachts. He and his daughter had been with me on a week-end cruise to St. George's, so that he knew his ropes. Very soon he developed into a first-class helmsman. He suffers, however, from the misfortune of deafness, and when at different ends of the boat we were unable to communicate with each other. We evolved a system of signs, which helped. He is a nephew of the late Lord Kitchener of Khartoum.

After unbending the cable and stowing the anchor below I felt that we were really at sea. Later in the afternoon several men-of-war were sighted ahead. The fleet had been out for exercises and was waiting to return to harbour. As we approached they formed into line, and, led by the Admiral, the *York*, *Dragon*, *Exeter*, and *Danae* steamed close under our stern. The Admiral hailed us through his megaphone, wishing us *bon voyage*, and officers and men of all the ships waved as they passed—a very cheering send-off.

Bermuda lies in latitude 32° north. During April the gale frequency (force 8 and above) is 4 to 5 per cent south of latitude 35° and 13 per cent to the northward. Towards the Azores these per-

centages decrease to 3 and 6 respectively. In May
the gale frequency is substantially less. For both
months the prevailing wind would be from north,
through west to south. We were unlikely to en-
counter much head-wind. I proposed, therefore,
to keep on the parallel of Bermuda until the end of
the month, and then to steer a direct course for
the Island of Fayal, which lies in $38\frac{1}{2}°$ N. Actually,
however, owing to steering courses on which the
ship would sail most easily and also to a pronounced current, we made a good course considerably to the northward of that proposed.

As the evening drew on the wind degenerated
into calms and light airs, so that by midnight we
had only made good twenty-three miles. I found
myself suffering mildly from a rather undistin-
guished complaint that made sitting at the helm
for long periods distinctly uncomfortable. The
suitable ointment was contained in the medicine
chest, and the affection yielded to treatment in a
few days.

Day succeeded day with little incident to relieve
the monotony; but no, monotony is wrong. What
with cooking, navigation, and sail-trimming there
was plenty to keep us busy. We could not risk
carrying away gear, but we drove the ship day and
night all we could without really pressing her. It
was on very few days that our run totalled less than
100 miles, and there was a tremendous satisfaction

in marking our position on the chart each day at noon. The memory of each day is now confused in my mind, but I have a recollection of the yacht continually straining forward and crashing, tearing her way through the seas as though eager, herself, to reach port. It was never seriously rough, and at no time did I have any real anxiety for the safety of the ship. The wind blew exactly as indicated by the pilot chart, changing from north to west and south, and then back again, varying in strength from light airs to a fairly strong wind. My log contains little beyond notes as to courses, sail shifting, and patent-log readings. On the 25th we saw a baby flying-fish skimming along the surface of the water. It was the only one we saw, and our hopes of fresh fish for breakfast were not fulfilled. On the 26th a large tanker passed us about a mile away. The same morning, while sailing with full mainsail and big staysail, we were struck by a violent squall. At the moment I was rather embarrassingly occupied below, and before I could come on deck the clew of the staysail had torn away from the sheet. We got down all sail and then set the reefed working staysail, under which we let the ship drive before it for some hours until the weather moderated at 11 A.M., when the mainsail could be set again.

In the evening I noted, 'Ship now knows where we want her to go'; evidently she was keeping her

course with the helm lashed. Next morning the
seizing wire securing the bowsprit to the bobstay
chafed through. This entailed a wet trip to the end
of the bowsprit to replace it. At 6 P.M., 'Sailing
magnificently with moderate beam sea, wind 4 to
5; cold, two-jersey weather; logging 5½ knots.'

Continually during this passage I was being surprised by the smallness of the seas in moderate or
fresh wind. On the trip out, twenty degrees farther
to the north, it had been just the other way; there
always seemed to be a big sea even in light winds.

On 28th April the wind drew aft, and for a few
hours the spinnaker was set, but the wind freshening, it had to come in, and the topsail was set on
the spinnaker boom in its place. The mainsail was
reefed at the same time, but the ship continued to
make good progress. By noon next day we had
made the best twenty-four-hour run since leaving
England, 147 miles. It was most exhilarating reeling off the knots like this; sea remained moderate,
nothing to worry about, though a few splashes
came into the cockpit. Careful steering, however,
was necessary. I gybed once and carried away the
boom guy. With only two on board it is very hard
work running before a fresh wind, and when careful steering is needed the four-hour watches seem
very long. What with navigation, food, &c., at least
half one's watch below is occupied. After two or
three days we felt the strain, and our tempers

suffered to some extent. But before any disaster took place the wind would shift and the ship would sail herself. We called that '*Emanuel*'s watch.' On several occasions we both got a full night's rest.

One must obviously reduce sail when running before a strong wind, and not have too much of the main-sheet out, so that a gybe may not be dangerous. Single-handed, one would lower the mainsail and drift along under headsails, making about two-thirds of the speed.

The spinnaker topping lift had rather a bad lead, and again chafed through. By the evening we were snugged down to the close-reefed mainsail, and staysail set across the deck. The following day, 30th April, we had made good another 140 miles, our position being from sights. It was rather surprising to find that in two days we had been set sixty miles to the north. The pilot chart shows a southerly current. The wind gradually became lighter; during the morning it was necessary to lower the mainsail to refit the parrel and the robands on the gaff. Chafe was also showing where the sail had rubbed on the backstays, and several seams needed stitching. The crew washed and shaved.

At 6 P.M., after gybing, we found the ship would sail herself, giving us a much-needed rest at the helm. I noted good reception on the wireless from U.S.A. stations, and a rather doubtful time signal. My chronometer watch had a rate of about half a minute a day, losing. The wireless set subsequently went dead, so that I was dependent on the watch for longitude.

For the next few days the wind remained light from the south, but sufficient for us to average over 100 miles a day. Most of this time little attention was needed at the helm, and I was able to get the big staysail repaired.

At 4 P.M. on 2nd May the patent log registered 907 miles—half-way. By the evening of 3rd May the wind had gone astern again, and was freshening. We continued with the big staysail set on the spinnaker boom, but in the small hours of the morning I was awakened by a gybe, and jumped to the cabin hatch. It was rather a wild night, wind force 6 to 7, and the ship was rolling violently. Everything seemed all right, and I shouted to Kitchener to carry on as he was steering, and then went below to light a cigarette before going forward to clear up. A plaintive voice called from the cockpit, 'Douglas, you are not going to leave me?' Poor Kitchener, I had not realised how confusing it must be, nor how easy for one with little experience to lose all sense of direction in the dark. I was up again in an instant and crawled forward. The spinnaker boom had pulled out from its gooseneck, which latter had fallen overboard. I secured the boom, and then between us we lowered the mainsail and staysail, leaving the ship to run under the middle jib. It was too hard work to continue running under a press of sail, and I did not wish to risk another gybe.

Next day the wind veered to the north and went light again. One of the jib-sheets was showing signs of chafe, so I cut out the bad place and knotted the ends. The mast-band had shifted, but was replaced without much difficulty. After making sail again the wind went altogether for some hours, leaving the yacht to roll idly in the swell, but at 6 P.M. I note, 'Sailing nicely, sails steadying us in the swell.'

But these pleasant conditions did not last for long. May 5th: '4 P.M., freshening to force 7 or 8 ; furled jib and five rolls in mainsail, though very little sea and sailing fairly comfortably with wind abeam.' The glass had fallen to 29.40, so before dark we got down the mainsail again. Under the reefed staysail the yacht was making a course of east by south. At 5 A.M. next morning I found she was heading south, so that there was some little doubt about the dead-reckoning position. At 6.30 A.M., while I was sitting in the cabin and Kitchener forward in his bunk, the startling roar of a syren burst on my ears. Looking out, I saw a large freighter approaching, and as she came close I read the name *Thistleford*. We carefully refrained from making any signal or gesture that might have been mistaken for a call for help, and she proceeded on her way. Later the wind took off sufficiently for the mainsail to be hoisted.

May 7th passed quietly, sailing comfortably with a light north-west wind. The lights of another ship were seen during the night several miles distant. We were crossing the track of ships bound to the West Indies or Gulf ports. Next day, 8th May, the wind piped up again. At 5.30 A.M., 'Small gale, down to reefed staysail and close-reefed mainsail. Noon, gale continues, force 7 to 8, ship steering herself, not much sea. 1 P.M. Fierce squalls and rain, followed by a lull; rolling heavily.' It was remarkable how comparatively little sea was raised by these strong winds. The breaking crests were quite inconsiderable, and we were able to continue sailing without serious discomfort. The sails steadied the ship, and as each wave rolled up on the beam *Emanuel* lifted bodily and then descended gently into the next hollow.

A day or two of light winds followed, mostly with an overcast sky, so that no sights for longitude were obtained after 7th May, when Fayal was 415 miles distant. I felt a trifle anxious approaching the vicinity of land, particularly as no great reliance could be placed on the time-keeper. On 9th May I got a good meridian altitude (sight for latitude), and so felt pretty confident that we should sight the Azores; but quite when

we should do so was uncertain. We felt it unwise
for both of us to sleep that night, and kept alter-
nate watches in the cabin. May 10th passed with
a strong south-west wind, and much rain and thick
weather, but during the afternoon the sun shone
out long enough to get a sight, which showed that
we were twenty-eight miles ahead of the reckoning. I had the succeeding middle watch (midnight to 4 A.M.). At 2 A.M. it came over very thick,
and I judged it unwise to continue through the
dark. Accordingly, the ship was hove-to, heading
back to the west. At 4.40 A.M. it was light, and
prudent to continue on our course, though the
visibility remained poor. The Azores are high,
with no outlying dangers.

At 8.20 A.M. Kitchener, who was then on
watch, called out 'Land.' There it lay, ahead of us,
the top of a mountain showing up above the clouds,
but at a considerable distance. A thrill that never
stales, and we had averaged 107 miles a day for
seventeen days. It had been a magnificent passage,
good progress every day, and never a moment's
anxiety.

By noon we were about four miles from Com-
prida Point at the western end of Fayal. With the
wind strong from the south, and a lumpy sea, it
was doubtful if we could weather the south shore.
Rather than make short tacks close to a lee shore,
I decided to run to leeward of the island, which

now seemed towering up above us from its summit of 3,000 feet. At first we made good progress, and it was most enjoyable feasting our eyes on the shore after having had nothing but sea to look at for several weeks. There appeared to be no beaches, rocky cliffs forming the coast-line, which then rose sharply on all sides to the central summit. All the ground appeared to be cut up into small patches of cultivation, which, with the absence of trees, gave the island rather an uninviting aspect. Many cottages were dotted about on the slopes.

Off Ribeirinha Point the wind failed, and darkness fell while we were in Fayal Channel, trying with indifferent success to make headway. Minor squalls were succeeded by calms, and there were some nasty-looking black clouds in the sky. These, however, came to nothing. Presently the lights of Horta showed up, and Magdalena Rocks could be seen through the dark on the eastern side of the channel. At last we could fetch the red light on the pier, and at 11 P.M. ghosted quietly into the harbour at Horta.

CHAPTER X

THE LAST STAGE

WE awoke next morning eager to see what sort of a place we had arrived at. Before us, looking more like a stage scene than reality, lay the town with its white houses on the slopes of the mountain. On the opposite side of the channel lay Pico, with its immense summit rising 7,600 feet high above the clouds.

Through the kindness of Mr. Fletcher, vice-consul and manager of the cable station, and of the other English residents, we spent a very enjoyable week in Horta. It was pleasant to stretch our legs on the country roads. Nearer acquaintance entirely changed our ideas as to the uninviting aspect of the island. In the valleys and on the heights were plenty of trees, but we were too early for the hydrangeas, for which the island is famous.

The summit of Pico was a continual challenge which, in company with Mr. and Mrs. Biggs of the cable station, we decided to accept. A motor-boat was chartered one afternoon to take us across the channel. Landing at Magdalena, we were met by the local innkeeper, who had engaged two guides for us. We started off in two motor-cars, which took us three or four miles into the foothills of the mountain. We had blankets and food with us, and, each shouldering a load, we started to ascend the grassy slopes. Presently we got above the clouds, and looked down on mile after mile of what appeared to be cotton-wool. A break in the clouds allowed us to see the distant harbour of Horta. Darkness fell, but we continued our climb with the help of the full moon, which rose with unexpected suddenness above the dark pile in front. The country was now becoming more rocky, and we soon found some caves, which are the usual half-way resting-place. We crawled through a tiny opening in the rocks and lay down in a low chamber. Our guides cut armfuls of heather for us to lie upon and made a huge fire. After eating our food we lay down for a few hours' rest. Our guides called us at 2 A.M., and we continued the climb. It was a lovely fine night, and in the bright light of the moon we could see our way almost as well as by day. All the grass had now been left behind, and we were ascending a steep slope of loose broken rocks and cinders. Here and there tufts of heather and other wiry shrubs gave good hold for the hands in places where it was necessary to scramble on hands and knees. Following on the heels of the guides the hours passed, and we became more and more exhausted. Inquiries as to how much farther were frequent.

Dawn was breaking as we at last reached the rim of the crater, which we followed for a quarter of a mile until we arrived at a spot where we could scramble down to its floor. The scene before us was like the imaginary pictures of the moon; black jagged rocks tumbled in utmost confusion and without any sign of vegetation. It was bitterly cold and in places ice had formed. Traversing the floor of the crater, we came to the foot of a steeple-shaped cone about 700 feet high. This occasioned a more difficult climb, scrambling from ledge to ledge of the loose rock. The sun had now risen above the horizon, with wonderful golden effect on the clouds below. At last we reached the top: a fairly level space about the size of a small room. The world, 7,000 feet below, seemed utterly remote. Perched upon the top of this needle-shaped spire I felt too utterly insecure, and promptly descended to the floor of the crater. For some time we had noticed clouds approaching, and in a few minutes we were enveloped in a thin mist and could see nothing. We had only just been in time to see the sun rise.

The return was much easier. We halted at the caves for breakfast and a couple of hours' rest, and then continued the descent until we picked up the cars at the end of the road.

On our arrival at Horta, Captain Liversage, of Messrs Bensaude & Co., had put his services at our disposal. He put through the paper-work at the customs, and his firm supplied us with most of our stores. A new chain-plate and a goose-neck for the spinnaker-boom were made, and the charges were most reasonable. I can heartily recommend any yachtsman to put himself in Captain Liversage's hands. The only snag about Portuguese ports is the customs and pilotage charges, which in *Emanuel's* case came to about two pounds. We did not actually take a pilot entering or leaving, but the morning after our arrival the pilot's motor-boat had towed us farther up the harbour.

On 18th May we embarked our last fresh provisions and prepared for sea. Business and farewells took much time, so that it was not till 5.30 P.M. that we weighed anchor and stood northward through the Fayal Channel for the open sea. We sailed past the western end of San Jorge during the dark, but could make out the outline of the high land easily enough. At daylight Graciosa was in sight to the north-east.

I left the Azores with regret, and should have liked to have spent several weeks exploring the islands. Kitchener, however, was in a fever to reach England. Also at my home the fruit-picking would soon be starting, and it seemed rather mean to leave my wife to cope with this single-handed for a second season.

By noon we had run seventy-four miles. The best

sailing route from the Azores to England runs northward for several hundred miles, when there is more likelihood of meeting steady westerly winds. As, however, the wind was from the north, I laid a direct course for the Scillies. We made a good run of 102 miles the next day, but then the wind dropped.

For the following six days we lay rolling in the swell with sails flapping uselessly. There would be occasional light airs from ahead, too light for the ship to sail herself, but not strong enough to make it worth while to sit at the helm. We slept and ate, and slept again, getting more and more impatient. At last, on the morning of 26th May, a light southerly wind sprang up. In good spirits again, we trimmed sail and set the spinnaker. By noon next day we had run 101 miles.

The wind remained with us from some westerly point till we reached England. Its force varied, sometimes strong, so that we ran under headsails alone, but mostly it was moderate, so that we could carry the mainsail with a reef in it.

On 3rd June we were in the mouth of the Channel and sighted several ships. The glass had been falling steadily, and there was a fresh wind with a big following sea. At noon sights showed that the Scilly Isles were about ninety miles ahead. A time signal from the telegraph station at Horta showed that the watch had been keeping a fairly steady

rate, but no great reliance could be put on it, and
I regretted very much that I had not been able to
repair the wireless set. By midnight we had run
another sixty miles, so that we expected to sight
the Bishop Light at any moment. The weather
looked very threatening, and the glass continued
to fall. The wind had drawn round to the south.
At 4 A.M. a violent squall with blinding rain struck
us. For the first time since leaving Bermuda I
felt anxious. Our position being uncertain, it was
possible that at any minute we might sight land
close to leeward, though by account we should be
ten miles southward of the Scilly Isles. But the
rain soon passed, and we watched the northern
horizon clearing. At 4.50 A.M. the low islands of
Scilly appeared bearing north-north-west about
ten miles distant. It was very pleasing to find ourselves just where we should have been. The wind
was now only a fresh breeze, but I did not like the
look of the very low glass. Here was shelter close
at hand, and it seemed advisable to make for it
rather than risk a gale so near the land. Putting
up the helm, we ran down towards the distant coast.
The Bishop Lighthouse showed up, and soon the
various headlands could be identified. We sailed
through St. Mary's Sound and brought up off
Hughtown at 7.30 A.M., seventeen days out from
Horta.

Good little *Emanuel*; how faithfully she has

served me! Although the Atlantic has frequently been crossed before by small craft, even from America to England by a dory, I think my ship is the smallest English yacht that has successfully made the round trip. I am not aware of any small craft that has made the voyage from Ireland to Newfoundland by the northern route.

There is not much more to tell. Hughtown received us with equanimity. Next morning, although the glass continued low, the weather looked fine. We weighed at 11.30 A.M. and continued up-Channel. The Wolf and then Land's End hove in sight, and how pleasant to see the well-remembered headlands again! We sailed by the Lizard in the dark and passed the Eddystone next morning, thence setting course for Prawle Point. Unfortunately the freshening wind backed south, and the weather became thick. We found ourselves close to the land and unable to weather Bolt Head. In the irregular Channel sea and with much reduced sail, *Emanuel* refused to go about, and by the time we had gybed we were uncomfortably close to the rocks. The tide would be soon turning against us, so I judged it safer to run back to Plymouth. It was now really very thick, and it was with much relief that we sighted the Mewstone and, later, Plymouth breakwater. For some days past we had been disappointed by our logged speeds, and on the present occasion *Emanuel* was handling particularly badly. It was not like her to miss stays as she had done off Bolt Head, and later we had considerable difficulty in making her pay off and gybe; in fact, she would not pay off until the main-sheet was eased right out. This was explained by the excessive growth of weeds and barnacles that was found on her bottom at Plymouth.

At 4 P.M. we anchored in the Cattewater. Next day it blew a gale from the south-west. My crew felt that the enforced inaction might quite possibly last for several days. I therefore persuaded him to leave me, which he did that afternoon. It was with much regret that we said good-bye to each other.

The next day the wind had eased to a moderate breeze, and I sailed out single-handed. Off the western end of the breakwater there was a sudden jerk and rasping noise. For a moment I could see nothing wrong, and thought that the bobstay had parted; then I noticed that the starboard after-shroud was slack. It had parted at the clip under the hounds. Before leaving Bermuda new rigging screws were fitted, which entailed re-splicing the lower end of each shroud. On the advice of the yacht yard I had fitted screw clips in the place of the usual wire seizings at the masthead. These clips had cut through the wire of the shrouds. It was *Emanuel*'s luck again that this had not happened off Bolt Head a couple of days before.

I let fly the peak halyards, gybed on to the other tack, and ran back into Plymouth Dock.

After making arrangements for new shrouds to be fitted, I took the train home. It was somewhat of an anti-climax to arrive at an empty house, my wife having gone down to Poole to meet me. A few days later I returned to Plymouth and sailed round to my mooring at Poole without incident.

CONCLUSIONS

It may be of interest to yachtsmen to put on record my general conclusions for handling a small craft in bad weather, though there is nothing original in them and it has all been said before. The most important fact that stands out in my mind is that heaving to is not the best way to sustain a real storm, by which I mean a wind of force 9 or 10. The sea will then be so heavy that the yacht will be thrown about in all directions, sometimes broadside on, sometimes head to wind. There will be a great strain on gear and hull, but more particularly the ship will be heeled over and in the worst position for withstanding the force of the breaking crests. *Emanuel* was once knocked completely flat by one of these when hove-to and flung bodily on her side to leeward. Were it not for her exceptional reserve of buoyancy, due to the wide cabin top, I think it conceivable that she might have capsized.

Up to winds of force 7 or 8 *Emanuel* will heave to very well and maintain her position to windward. She rides very comfortably owing to the steadying action of her sails.

With stronger winds there are three courses open: (1) to lie a-try—*i.e.*, with all sail down, the ship drifting where she will; (2) to run before the wind; and (3) to lie to a sea-anchor. With regard to the first, the ship will lie broadside on to the seas, and will ride buoyantly over the waves, but the top of each one will slop over the stern, not necessarily with great force, but enough water will come on board to endanger a vessel with a large open cockpit. Every now and then, perhaps twice every two hours, the yacht will happen to be at the top of a wave, when its crest breaks with especial violence.

During the great storm of 15th to 17th November, wind force 9 or 10, I remember watching the seas and trying particularly to gauge the actual height of the breaking crests. It was nothing like one-third of their height, as I have seen mentioned in one of the logs printed in the *R.C.C. Journal*, but as far as I could judge about five feet. This does not sound very much, but was sufficiently terrifying in practice. The shock of such a breaker striking the ship was very great. I estimated the total height of the waves as thirty to forty feet and their length as 500 feet. The tops of the waves did not just fall forward in a smother of foam, but definitely curled over and fell like breakers on a beach. I have a vivid remembrance of one particular wave. As the yacht lay broadside on in the trough of the sea, a huge crest many feet above me curled over and broke; just below and behind the curling tip I could see the green curve of unbroken water. This particular wave spent its force before it reached me, but I did wonder very much what would happen if such a mass of water should actually fall on the ship. I was on the edge of the Gulf Stream, which accounted probably for the very confused state of the sea, the waves approaching from varying angles. The advancing faces of the waves were very steep; I will not say they were almost vertical, but it was very remarkable to see such a very steep slope of water, and one wondered that a greater part of the wave did not break. Another remarkable sight was the pinnacle effect of the waves. Here and there the tops would rise up in points with almost the steepness of a church spire to a height of perhaps six feet above the general level of the wave; sometimes these pin-nacles broke and sometimes they did not. I do not wish to convey the idea that this storm was anything beyond the usual experience of those regularly crossing the Atlantic in the winter, but my opportunities for observing it were rather unusual.

The size and steepness of the waves seemed entirely un-important as long as the crest did not happen to break on to the ship; she appeared to ride over them equally well which-ever way she was pointing.

When the breaking crest becomes so big that one fears the deck or sides may be stove in, one should endeavour to get one end of the ship pointed to the seas as in (2) or (3). I do not think that it matters much which end, provided, of course, that the stern is watertight. The pointed ends of the ship will offer much less resistance to the breaking seas than the ship's side, and a ship's hull is probably stronger in re-sisting a blow from end to end than athwartships. She can also recoil more readily from a shock which is in the direc-tion of her length.

The ship will lie more comfortably if head to wind at a sea-anchor, since the cabin doors can be left open without heavy splashes driving down below, but the question of a riding sail is a difficulty for a cutter, which I have already discussed in Chapter VII. I have twice before had occasion to lie to a sea-anchor: once was in H. Klugh's *Sandhopper*, and the occasion is described in the *R.C.C. Journal* for 1907. It was during a passage across the North Sea, and the yacht, a centre-board yawl of four tons, lay in perfect safety and in fair comfort with her mizzen set. The other occasion was a few years later, and ended in the loss of my four-ton cutter, *Vixen*, in the neighbourhood of the Galloper Sand. Without some riding sail I do not think that any yacht will lie head to wind at a sea-anchor; at least not to one of a size that can be practically carried on board. In each of the three yachts, the sea-anchor had no observable effect until some sail aft was hoisted. To improvise a riding sail is not so easy as it sounds. During the gale of 7th November it had seemed an impossible effort to set a jib aft until there happened to be a lull. I got it up then, tack to the counter, head on the peak halyards, and the clew lashed to the rail on the cabin top. It was a new sail of very heavy canvas, roped all the way round, but cut very full. When the wind resumed its previous violence, the yacht rode very well, but as I have previously described, every now and then she would come exactly head to wind and the sail would flog. I tried again and again to tauten everything up, but without result, and the viciousness with which it flapped to and fro can hardly be described. The whole ship quivered from the jerks. I do not know whether it would be possible to prevent this flogging in a flatter sail nor whether accurate adjustment of its size and position would enable a ship to ride with the sea a little on the bow without actually coming head to wind. Accurate adjustments are not too easy, however, under the conditions in which a sea-anchor is needed. It is partly a moral difficulty; one becomes cowed and inert from the prolonged noise and motion, so that the slightest exertion seems an enormous effort.

If (2) is adopted, the ship must be got before the wind and stern hawsers put out. I put an old motor tyre and some coils of rope on the end of one and the broken half of the main boom on the other. There did not seem any very great strain on them. *Emanuel* then seemed fairly safe. My memory of the great storm is now rather blurred, and my log only contains a few brief notes as to the direction of the ship's drift. I have no recollection of the yacht receiving any very severe shocks after she had been put before the wind. The blows that I do remember were when she was hove-to or a-try. I do remember lying on the counter to parcel the hawsers and spluttering and shaking my head after a sea had washed over me, but there had been no great weight of water in it; and when getting the second hawser out I remember a heavy splash knocking me to the lee side of the cockpit; but neither of these were in any way serious. I have a hazy recollection of seeing one large breaker curling over from the port quarter and jumping into the cabin to avoid it.

At no time did there appear to be any particular strain on the rudder; the tiller was always lashed.

I have recently seen an article in an American yachting paper where a diagram is given of how a yacht turned head over heels. I do not know what a ship might do if she were running fast and was carried forward on the advancing face of a big wave; but with her stern hawsers out *Emanuel* showed little tendency to be carried forward: she lifted and allowed the waves to pass her with great deliberation. I had no anxiety that she might not keep the right way up. She rode best with the head of the staysail hoisted three or four feet above the deck, the rest of the sail being lashed down to the bowsprit.

From the foregoing it would seem that it is entirely unnecessary ever to heave to with a fair wind, however hard it blows. Whether such a conclusion would hold good for other yachts I cannot say. Conor O Brien says that he has never hove *Saoirse* to with a fair wind. *Tai-Mo-Shan*, however, hove to in a westerly gale when on passage from Bermuda to England. With a bigger ship than *Emanuel* it might be difficult to reduce the speed sufficiently for safety even under bare poles.

The old controversy about speed when running never seems to get settled, and has recently cropped up again in the yachting Press. Parry, the Arctic explorer, speaks, over one hundred years ago, of setting more sail to keep before the seas. A present captain in the Navy with long experience of destroyers, when discussing a great gale off the Azores, was rather horrified when I suggested that it might have been better to ease down to five knots instead of to fourteen. Different types of ships need different handling, but I am not convinced. I prefer to remain in company with Dr. Worth, Captain Voss, and others, who believe that the chief factor of safety lies in getting the way off the ship. Many other factors, of course, are present when considering large steamships.

On arrival at Bermuda I was able to compare my notes with the ship's logs; the wind velocities as read at the meteorological station are also published in the local Press. For five days I had been running before a wind of force 7 or 8. The sea was heavy and the motion uncomfortable, but at no time during this period did it appear at all dangerous, nor did the crests become very large. The seas were much more regular than during the bad weather of a few days previously. After sighting the North Rock beacon the ship was quite manageable, and would definitely go to windward, though only very slowly. She was somewhat crippled by the loss of the boom, which prevented the mainsail from setting to its best advantage.

I do not remember, either on this cruise or on any previous one, ever having found it necessary to steer *Emanuel* with special regard to individual waves, though I may often enough have put the helm one way or the other to avoid a splash. Before it was essential to luff up or bear away for the big ones I would heave to or reduce sail; though, of course, there might be occasions, such as clawing off a lee shore, when this procedure might be imperative.

Once, while at Bermuda, I had occasion to sail across the enclosed waters of the sound when it was blowing hard. The recorded wind velocity was an average of forty-seven miles per hour with gusts up to sixty-one. As the water was sheltered there was no sea; *Emanuel* was under close-reefed mainsail and reefed staysail, and was towing a heavy dinghy. Under these conditions she could work to windward, but had to be handled with care to avoid missing stays.

APPENDIX II

STORE LIST PROVIDED FOR THE BANTRY-NEWFOUNDLAND PASSAGE

FORE CABIN, STARBOARD LOCKER

24 Tins Stews.	1 Quart Methylated Spirit.
8 ,, Sausages.	Sextant.
8 ,, Soup.	Patent Log.
6 ,, Russian Salad.	Box of Red and White Flares.
27 ,, Bully Beef.	Tin of Medicines.
5 ,, Crayfish.	Spare Lamp Glasses.

FORE CABIN, PORT LOCKER

18 Tins Fruit.	12 Tins Sardines.
8 ,, Salmon.	12 ,, Cream.
8 ,, Asparagus.	12 ,, Milk.
2 ,, Prawns.	6 ,, Tongues.
7 lb. Brazil Nuts.	8 ,, Peas.
10 ,, Rice.	12 lb. Flour.
3 ,, Coffee.	1 Tin Salt.
10 ,, Sugar.	1 Bottle Whisky.
1 Jar Pickles.	1 gal. Methylated Spirit.
1½ lb. Tea.	½ ,, Olive Oil.

MAIN CABIN, No. 1 DRAWER, PORT

4 Packets Dates.	2 Boxes Dried Figs.
2 lb. Raisins.	2 lb. Sultanas.

APPENDIX II

MAIN CABIN, No. 2 DRAWER, PORT

2 Packets Matches.	2 Bars Salt.
2 lb. Candles.	4 Bottles Oxo.
2 ,, Tobacco.	4 Pots Meat Paste.
500 Cigarettes.	2 Tins Mixed Spice.
1 lb. Cocoa.	2 Bottles Salad Cream.

MAIN CABIN, No. 3 DRAWER, PORT
Fresh Vegetables and Fruit for Ready Use.

MAIN CABIN, MONEY DRAWER

7 Spare Bulbs for Torches.	Pencils, Ink, Gum, and Sundries.
1 Spare W.T. Fuse Bulb.	Sixpence halfpenny.

MAIN CABIN, No. 1 DRAWER, STARBOARD
Ready Use Groceries.

MAIN CABIN, No. 2 DRAWER, STARBOARD
3 Loaves × 2 lb.

MAIN CABIN, No. 3 DRAWER, STARBOARD

4 Bottles Honey.	15 Eggs.

MAIN CABIN, STARBOARD BUNK LOCKER

Hawser.	10 Old Tins Meat, &c.

MAIN CABIN, PORT BUNK LOCKER

Ship's Legs.	2 Dozen Bottles Beer.

FORECASTLE

Lamps.	1 Lifebuoy.
Skylight Cover.	Sea-anchor.
2 Life Jackets.	Chain Locker.

ROUGH PASSAGE

Cockpit Locker, Starboard

3 × 7 lb. Tins Cabin Biscuits. | Spare Blocks.
6 lb. Silverside of Beef. | Boatswain's Gear.

Cockpit Locker, Port

2 Gem Water Tins × 2¾ gal. | 2 × 7 lb. Tins Cabin Biscuits
3 Cans Paraffin × 2 gal. | 8 Wooden Wedges.

Cockpit Locker, Aft

20 lb. Potatoes. | 5 lb. Turnips.
7 ,, Onions. | Lead and Copper Sheeting.
2 dozen Bananas. | Oakum and Caulking
8 Grape Fruit. | Cotton.
1 dozen Oranges. | Spare Sails.

Box on Top of Cabin

4 Dozen Eggs in Jar. | 4 lb. Beef in Brine.

Meat Safe on Cabin Top

5 lb. Bacon. | 7 lb. Butter.
5 ,, Ham. | 2 ,, Dripping.
2½ ,, Cheese. | 4 ,, Fresh Meat.

APPENDIX III

ABSTRACTS FROM *EMANUEL*'S LOG

Bantry to St John's

Date.	Lat. Obs.	Lat. D.R.	Long. Obs.	Long. D.R.	Run.	Remarks.
May						
26	51 36N	—	9 50W	—	15	7.45 A.M. weighed.
27	—	51 37N	12 5W	—	84	—
28	51 38	51 46	13 18	13 15	45	—
29	51 47	51 40	14 04	14 04	30	—
30	52 07	51 53	16 07	15 57	80	—
31	52 30	52 30	18 42	18 34	97	Passed s.s. *Fishpool.*
June						
1	52 34	52 37	20 11	19 58	54	—
2	52 23	52 19	23 14	23 09	112	Washed.
3	—	51 52	—	26 04	109	Gale.
4	—	52 12	—	28 34	94	Pooped.
5	52 52	52 18	28 55	29 34	42	
6	—	53 12	—	30 39	67	Gale.
7	52 57	53 10	31 56	31 59	49	— —
8	—	52 44	34 59	—	111	—
9	52 03	51 46	—	37 16	94	Washed.
10	51 14	51 12	—	39 38	101	—
11	50 40	50 30	40 52	40 45	58	Broadcast from St. John's.
12	—	49 40	—	42 01	76	Gale.
13	—	49 39	—	44 09	83	—
14	—	49 21	—	46 35	97	Fog.
15	49 18*	49 12	—	47 11	25	—
16	—	48 28	—	48 42	72	—
17	—	48 23	—	48 55	10	—
18	—	48 15	—	50 23†	60	Iceberg passed.
19	—	—	—	—	100	4.15 P.M. anchored St. John's.
					1765	

* Last sight for latitude.
† Longitude sight, P.M., put ship 27 miles to eastward.

215

ROUGH PASSAGE

St. John's to Bermuda, 1934

Date.	Lat. Obs.		Lat. D.R.		Long. Obs.		Long. D.R.		Run.	Remarks.
Nov.										
3	—		—		—		—		—	2 P.M. sailed.
4	—		46	15N	—		52	55W	83	Very cold.
5	44	56N	45	02	53	06W	52	59	79	—
6	—		44	24	54	05	53	49	52	—
7	—		43	05	—		55	16	94	Full gale, sea-anchor.
8	43	18	43	23	56	7	55	49	38	Daventry time signal.
9	42	55	42	52	56	2	56	34	26	Fell overboard in calm.
10	—		42	02	—		56	46	62	Gale, hove-to.
11	40	50	40	55	57	54	58	03	88	—
12	—		40	01	—		58	29	56	Gale, sea-anchor.
13	—		40	23	—		58	08	27	—
14	39	04	39	24	—		58	16	80	Reefing gear broke; set trysail.
15	—		38	35	—		59	19	58	Storm.
16	—		38	20	—		59	36	21	Storm.
17	38	25	38	03	—		59	14	18	Calm.
18	38	07	38	14	57	22	59	19	89	Calm.
19	37	39	37	40	56	39	56	58	45	Calm.
20	37	09	37	36	56	54	56	43	32	Calm; bathed.
21	—		36	47	—		57	24	33	Easterly gale for next five days.
22	—		35	47	—		59	10	106	—
23	35	07	34	51	—		60	05	61	—
24	—		33	53	—		61	39	112	—
25	33	15	32	58	—		63	07	80	—
26	32	22	32	36	64	57	63	22	{ 108 / 20 }	} 3 P.M. anchored Ely's Harbour.
									1468	

St. John's to Bermuda direct, 1072 miles.
Average effective speed, 47 miles per day.

BERMUDA TO AZORES

Date.	Lat. Obs.	Lat. D.R.	Long. Obs.	Long. D.R.	Run.	Remarks.
April						
24	32 22N	—	64 39W	—	7	9.30 A.M. sailed.
25	—	32 31	—	63 5W	80	—
26	33 34	33 17	—	61 08	118	—
27	—	34 03	58 37	58 50	129	—
28	34 27	34 32	57 02	56 51	82	—
29	—	35 00	—	54 03	147	Best day's run.
30	36 54	35 54	52 22	51 36	140	—
May						
1	36 53	37 00	50 02	50 13	113	—
2	36 47	36 35	47 53	47 56	102	—
3	36 44	36 23	45 27	45 44	117	—
4	—	37 14	—	43 12	112	—
5	—	37 40	—	41 52	84	—
6	38 24	37 41	40 06	39 51	94	—
7	39 04	38 54	37 41	37 38	120	—
8	—	38 57	—	35 51	86	—
9	38 46	38 31	—	34 02	86	—
10	—	38 39	—	31 14	132	—
11	38 38	38 23	28 54	29 25	110	—
					20	11 P.M. anchored in Horta.
					1879	

Total set 181 miles north, 10 miles east.
Average speed, 107 miles per day.

AZORES TO SCILLY

Date.	Lat. Obs.	Lat. D.R.	Long. Obs.	Long. D.R.	Run.	Remarks.
May						
18	—	—	—	—	—	5.30 P.M. sailed.
19	39 9N	—	27 20W	—	74	—
20	—	40 12N	—	20 35W	102	—
21	40 24	40 24	24 33	24 46	49	—
22	40 26	40 27	23 40	23 31	41	—
23	40 31	40 26	—	23 20	16	—
24	40 29	40 42	22 4	22 28	58	—
25	40 38	40 54	22 12	21 54	11	—
26	40 46	40 47	21 50	21 47	19	176 miles made good in 6 days.
27	—	41 23	—	19 46	101	—
28	—	41 48	—	18 10	77	—
29	43 20	42 49	16 43	16 47	113	—
30	44 30	44 33	—	15 24	90	—
31	45 17	45 14	13 28	13 26	95	—
June						
1	—	46 03	—	11 52	81	—
2	47 33	47 20	09 51	09 44	123	—
3	49 7	48 56	8 9	7 47	116	—
4	—	—	—	—	88	7.30 A.M. anchored Hughtown.
					1254	

Total set 33 miles north, 7 miles west.
Average speed, 76 miles per day.

THE
ADVENTURE OF THE
FAEROE ISLANDS

An Account of a Voyage to the
Faeroe Islands in a Seven-Tonner

BY

M. HELEN GRAHAM
With notes by Commander R. D. Graham

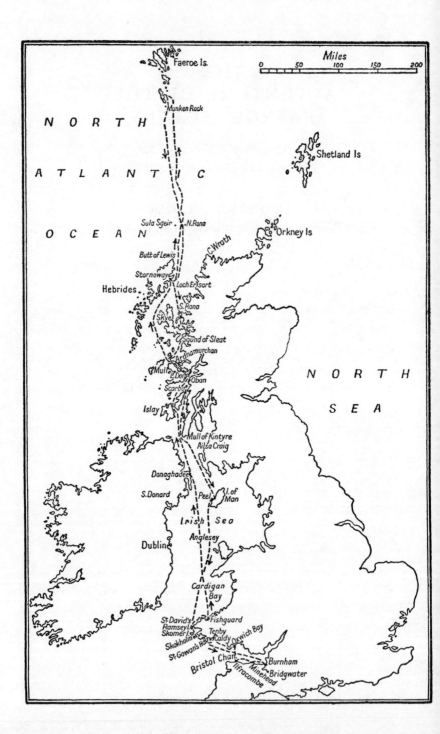

PREFACE

THE Faeroe Islands have been described as the most out-of-the-way archipelago in the world. This statement, although perhaps an exaggeration, contains a vein of truth. Remote islands in the Pacific are visited by scientific expeditions, and the wilds of New Guinea are described by experienced travellers. The Faeroes, from their proximity to our shores, do not attract such as these, while the usually rough sea passage, and entire lack of tourist facilities in the islands themselves, prevent the access of ordinary visitors. Our trawlers fish off the surrounding banks, and often run in for shelter between the islands, but their crews are not given to writing.

The group lies almost half-way between Scotland and Iceland, and occupies a space of some 60 miles N. and S., and 40 miles E. and W. The total area is 540 square miles, the larger islands being comparable in size to the Isle of Wight.

The population is about 20,000, descendants of the original Norse settlers of a thousand years ago. Although governed by Denmark, they cling tenaciously to their own customs and language. The latter, akin to, but distinct from Icelandic, has only been put into writing in quite recent years, and would probably offer much of interest to the philologist. It is now taught in their schools, and one of their grievances against their Danish rulers has been removed.

Sheep farming, fishing, and fowling are the principal occupations. There appears to be an entire lack of any class distinctions, and while no one is rich, and life must be hard, we saw no signs of real poverty or want.

The climate is extremely wet, and even in August we found it necessary to keep a stove going in the cabin most of the day. My daughter suffered, not indeed from frostbite, but from chilblains.

The narrative which follows has been compiled by my daughter from her diary and the ship's log. I have added a few technical notes, which it is hoped may be of interest to yachtsmen.

R. D. GRAHAM

Stawell,
 Bridgwater.

THE ADVENTURE OF THE
FAEROE ISLANDS

DURING the evening of 1st August, 1929 *Emanuel*
passed through Bridgwater dock gates into the
muddy waters of the river Parrett. The crew consisted of Commander R. D. Graham, my father,
skipper, the writer, his daughter, as mate, and an
Oxford undergraduate as crew. It was a beautiful
evening, and there was little or no wind. Some
boys on the river bank towed *Emanuel* a short
distance, and the tide took her a little farther, but
about half a mile beyond the dock gates she
grounded on the mud, and all attempts to get her
off with the kedge were unsuccessful. We therefore had supper, and turned in.

Next morning we were under way about 5 A.M.,
but stuck again a mile or two farther on. In the
afternoon we floated, and at last cleared the river
bar. There was a fresh breeze blowing, and a slight
chop in the channel, nothing very much, but
enough to make *Emanuel* quite lively. I was below
resting as we drew out of Burnham, and when I
came on deck I found the crew looking rather
green and unhappy. It was his first experience of
yachting, other than on the Broads, so it was not

surprising. The skipper was not looking too gay, either, and asked me to get some biscuits. The biscuits were in the forecastle, and I took some time getting at them; as some paraffin had upset, and smelt very strongly, when I returned to the deck I felt rather queer, too. Crew and skipper had both been feeding the fishes, and I soon followed their example—a good beginning for a cruise! The situation was really rather humorous, though at the actual time it did not strike us as such. Hush! 'tell it not in Gath, publish it not in the streets of Ashkelon,' but I had never seen skipper seasick before, and he was more upset than I. Perhaps seasickness affects age more than youth, for I was not as ill as either of my companions, and took a spell at the helm while the crew retired to my bunk (the most comfortable in the ship), and skipper lay down on his own.

We reached Minehead about 10 P.M., and anchored under Greenaley point, an old friend of ours. Some five years ago I tried to sketch this point, and as far as I remember the result rather pleased me at the time. The other day a piece of paper, with some weird blobs of paint on it, turned up. It was obviously meant to be a painting of sorts, but what? Surely we had never seen anything that resembled the smudges on that page. Suddenly it dawned on me. It was my sketch of Greenaley point. I blushed, and hastily tore it up.

Skipper was up early next morning, and got under way single handed. I joined him later, and we had breakfast. There was enough wind to necessitate a reef in the mainsail. The sun shone, and we had a glorious sail to Ilfracombe. Yesterday's performance was not repeated by skipper or myself, though the crew did not appear till we had anchored in the outer harbour at about 10.15 A.M. We stowed the sails, and made everything shipshape, and then set to and had our first substantial meal for thirty-six hours. After that, having more or less recovered, the crew and I went ashore to shop, and left skipper to wash up. Later we were towed into the inner harbour, and made fast alongside the quay. After supper a friend of the skipper came on board, and we had a very pleasant evening.

There was some talk of going out early on Sunday morning, but the weather looked so bad that we decided to wait. Eventually we left Ilfracombe at 4.30 P.M., and had a fine sail across the Channel. It was the first time crew had not felt seasick. We approached the Welsh shore when it was getting dark, and it seemed to me that we were very close to the rocks. The breakers roared angrily, and once I could have sworn I saw a line of foam, though I admit I may have imagined it. At last we anchored in Oxwich Bay, in the early hours of the morning, and turned in for a brief sleep. Skipper and crew were up early, and I joined them for breakfast. There was a slight sea, and crew had to eat his egg on deck. After breakfast both men turned in, and I sailed *Emanuel* towards Caldy.

When we drew close to the island, skipper came on deck, and we anchored in Caldy Road about noon. We stretched our legs on the island, and then returned. The weather did not look promising, but we sailed up to the entrance of the Sound to have a look at things. Skipper's log records, 'N.B.G.' My own diary is milder, it says, 'Not worth going out'; but we both meant the same. We returned to Tenby, berthed alongside the jetty, and went ashore to the pictures.

Next morning, 6th August, skipper and crew got under way early. I turned out about 6 A.M. I would remark, at this point, that a naval officer's log is supposed to be an accurate account of the sailing of his ship, at least that is what I have always imagined. On this occasion, however, I read in our skipper's log, 'Smell of breakfast cooking induced mate to turn out.' This was *not* accurate; in fact, it was quite wrong, for a sudden feeling that if she did not go on deck *instanter* she'd be seasick, was the real inducement. However, she managed to eat some breakfast, and soon was perfectly all right again. Skipper has since rectified his error.

By the time we had rounded St. Gowan's, we found we could steer our course up the Irish Sea, and so decided to go on. Crew was below sleeping. The conditions for making a passage were good, and to put into Milford Haven, as had been our original plan, seemed a mere waste of time. Skokholm and Skomer were visible ahead, and after giving instructions as to the course to be steered, skipper went below for a rest. I told crew about our change in plans, and disillusioned him about going into Milford. He seemed a bit surprised, but said nothing. Presently, when Skomer was abeam, skipper came up, and then I nearly fell overboard with surprise, for crew asked skipper to put him ashore at Fishguard. Apparently seasickness had been too much for him. *Emanuel* had nearly stood on her head when passing through St. Gowan's race that morning. Skipper went below to look at charts, etc., and discovered that the glass had taken a sharp turn downwards. Accordingly, we decided to go in to Ramsey Sound, and land crew at St. David's Head. We anchored in a little bay,[1] where we saw two French fishing-boats. We went across to these Frenchmen, and asked for some fish for supper. They supplied us with fish, and also a rabbit. Skipper was very pleased with himself, because he knew what 'un

[1] The anchorage is just north of the Bitches. With a north-going tide a vessel will be swept past; but on standing close in to Ramsey Island one finds an eddy which will take her to the anchorage.

lapin' was. No payment would be accepted, and so we gave them some beer. Beer is a very useful thing to have on board, for fishermen gladly accept it in lieu of payment. The Frenchmen were very hospitable and friendly. They said they had noticed me at the helm when entering, and we caught the words 'matelot' and 'soldat.' I hope the latter was not applied to me. Very kindly, they agreed to land crew next morning.

Skipper and I went for a row before breakfast. We tried to land, but were unable to scale the cliffs. As a matter of fact, I think if a horde of savages had been after us we would have climbed up easily enough. The shore is very weather-beaten and eaten away. We rowed right into one cave, where the waves thundered in a most alarming and threatening manner. We were glad to get out into the sunlight again. After breakfast we landed at the proper landing-stage and walked round the Island. We had a glorious view from the top, Grassholm, the Smalls, and Bishop being visible in the distance. After lunch the Frenchmen called for crew, and he departed.

We left Ramsey about 5, and a light, northerly breeze enabled us to reach Fishguard by the evening, and we anchored for the night. Early next morning, 8th August, we left Fishguard. During the first part of the morning there was hardly any wind, and so we had an opportunity of taking some snaps of *Emanuel*. There is something very thrilling about a ship under sail, and *Emanuel* is a beautiful sight with the sunlight gleaming on her white sails. After lunch we picked up a westerly breeze, and soon were racing along at six knots, course north, up the Irish Sea.[1] At last we were making real headway. The last week had been very slow, but hard work.

I turned out about 3 A.M., and presently, in the dim distance, made out the Mourne Mountains and Slieve Donard, showing faintly against the pink sky of dawn. The breeze held till we reached the South Rock Light vessel at dusk,[2] when it fell, and left us to roll in the swell, and get damp in the mist, which soon developed into proper rain. There was a thick fog and rain most of the night. The sea remained like oil. Early next morning a light air enabled us to reach Donaghadee, where we anchored. We spent most of the day clearing up on board. Some friends from Belfast came to tea, and took us for a drive afterwards. There was talk about going on in the evening, but the weather was wet, and we were tired, at least I was, for I could only just keep my eyes open during supper.

The next day, Sunday, we left Donaghadee, still

[1] Bardsey Island abeam about nine miles at 8.43 P.M.

[2] At noon, patent log gave 122·5 miles in previous twenty-four hours. This is *Emanuel*'s best day's run so far.

bound north.[1] It was very exciting, making out the Mull of Kintyre and Ailsa Craig, our first glimpses of Scotland. Next morning we sailed through Islay Sound. We passed some fascinating-looking islands called 'Isles of the Sea,' a charming and appropriate name. They were wee islets, jagged, and scarred by the waves. The surf breaking on the rocks formed a ring of white to protect their shores from the blue waters of the deep.

We sailed into the entrance of Mull Sound. The scenery was wonderful, and formed a great contrast to the 'green hills o' Somerset,' that we were accustomed to. We anchored in Loch Don, and went ashore for milk, which we were very kindly given, the cow being specially milked for us. We obtained a lovely view over the Lochs, the purple, heather-clad mountain-tops toning down through all shades to the vivid blue of the water below. Later in the evening we beat up to Ardtonish Bay, anchored, had supper, and turned in.

Next morning we sailed through the Sound of Mull, and headed for the western extremity of Skye. We spent the night at sea. When I turned out, about 2.30 A.M., it began to rain. It's a curious fact that it always rains during my watch. The rain came down in torrents, and I must admit I was not keeping a very good look-out. Unless one stood

---

[1] Mate was instructed in use of sextant, but would use the index glass as a mirror in which to admire herself.

up, the dinghy blocked the starboard view. Suddenly there was a swishing of water, and a little drifter shot across our bows, yelled a cheery 'good morning,' and was past. What a shock she gave me. I thought we had run on a reef, or something, at least. As we neared Stornoway we saw swarms of drifters entering the harbour. We beat in with a light air, which left us as we got near the top, and we had to sweep the yacht across the harbour, right through the stream of fishing-boats. No doubt some of them were annoyed, but they made us roll in their wakes. We had tea ashore, and later on saw a man-of-war anchor; we also watched the arrival of the mail boat, the great event of the day at Stornoway. This time she brought with her crowds of fisher girls, who had come for the herrings, from the mainland. Some fishermen said we were mad, or at least implied it, to think of going to the Faeroes!

August 15th was our first day without sailing. We spent the morning shopping, and in the afternoon called on H.M.S. *Rosemary* for a chronometer comparison. It was a good excuse, I could see skipper was longing to go aboard a man-of-war again. We were very hospitably received, and stayed to tea and dinner. Next morning we had lunch in the *Rosemary*, and then took their pilot, Lieut. H. L. Jenkins, for a sail to Loch Erisort. We had a delightful sail, and the view across Loch

Erisort was very beautiful. Saturday's weather was too bad for sailing. H.M.S. *Flinders*, which had come in, invited us on board, so we went, and met with a very kind reception.

Sunday, 18th August, saw us really bound for the Faeroes. We left after breakfast, and actually had the sun out. As we sailed north the coast-line before the Butt came up, and dipped again. I slept in the afternoon, and by the time I came up once more the Butt was faintly discernible behind.

'Shall we go on?' asked skipper.

'Rather,' I replied; and so we went on. We made good progress, and by Tuesday morning were expecting land at any moment.[1]

---

[1] AUGUST 18th.—Weighed 8.30 A.M., light N. wind, and reached northward along coast; 9.0, streamed P.L.; noon, P.L. 13; 2.0 P.M., freshening. Lowered topsail, 3.45 P.M., off Butt of Lewis, co. N.N.E. by E., 8.30. Between Sula Sgeir and N. Rona, co. N. by E. Made good from 3.45, 29¼ m. P.L. 30 m., so latter fairly accurate, allowing for yawing. 8.0 P.L. 54¾. I relieved mate at 11 P.M.; she reported passing through a fleet of drifters off N. Rona.

AUGUST 19th.—Midnight, P.L. 88½, wind W.S.W., freshening; hove to and reefed. 2.30 A.M.—Unrolled mainsail. 3.0 A.M. —Mate took charge. 6.0—I relieved mate; more or less continuous drizzle all night. 8.0 A.M.—P.L. 109½; light airs only.

Noon—P.L. 117½, 0.42 P.M. obs. pos. 60 deg. 3′ N., 6 deg. 24′ W., 8 miles S.E. from D.R. 4.0 p.m.—P.L. 133; drizzle continues. 8.0—P.L. 147; mate slightly indisposed, so order her to keep below; hove to for supper, and then steered N. to avoid gybing, the wind being more to the southward.

AUGUST 20th.—0 P.M. (midnight)—P.L. 167; wind freshening; hove to; reefed mainsail, and stowed jib. A wet half-hour on the

It was very foggy; there was no wind, and a vile, irregular swell. Skipper's sights put him out of his dead-reckoning position, so we sounded, and eventually, after connecting all the thin line on board, and sticking grease on to the end of the lead,[1] we

---

foc'stle. I changed into dry clothes, ate some food, and then lay down for two or three hours, thinking it quite safe to leave the yacht unattended in this lonely part of the ocean. 3.25 A.M.—Let draw; course N.E. by N., estimated drift N.W. 5 m. 4.0 A.M.—P.L. 171; wind light; unrolled mainsail and set jib. 6.0 A.M.—Put the helm up for a heavy sea, and gybed mainsail. The sheet fouled the P.L., and carried away the shoe, but the lanyard prevented loss of the instrument. 6.30 A.M.—Mate recovered; mist; visibility ¼-mile. 9.0 A.M.—Munken Rock bore N. by E. 5 miles by D.R., but visibility very poor, and nothing in sight. A glimpse of the sun enabled me to get a sight which put us 15 miles to west of D.R. position. This was subsequently proved wrong, owing to bad horizon.

9.30 A.M.—It was now so thick we could only see three or four ship's lengths. Although not much wind, there was a steep, irregular sea, overrunning a heavy ground sea. It seemed unsafe to approach the land under such conditions, so hove to on port tack, heading W. A sounding at 6.0 P.M. showed we were on the banks, confirming what we had supposed from the state of the sea. 10.45—Slightly clearer; steered N.E., expecting to make land at any minute. Sea much smoother, suggesting deeper water. In very serious doubt as to our position.

2.0 P.M.—Mate spotted land on port beam, and in a few minutes we were able to identify the high land of Suderö and the Dimons. 2.30—a/c N.W. 3.10—Little Dimon N.W. ¼W. 12 m. by vert angle. Off entrance to Trangisvaag, the wind headed us, and came in puffs, but as the fiord is practically free from danger there was no difficulty in beating up.

6.0 p.m.—Anchored on N.E. side of fiord just above Tvaeraa, in 15 fm. Made good from Stornoway 214 miles.

[1] Arming.

brought up a piece of shell. We concluded that we had struck the bottom at a depth of about sixty fathoms. It was not until the afternoon that we sighted land, and then it was to port, instead of starboard. However, we turned round and headed for it. As we drew near we gradually made out the entrance to Trangisvaag.

The coast-line was very high and mountainous. There was a magnificent cliff, at the entrance to the fiord, which rose sheer out of the sea until it was lost in the clouds that hung over the hills. As we sailed up the fiord we were struck with the quaint, foreign appearance of the houses. There were also some curious beehive-shaped lumps here and there along the shore. We could not imagine what they were.[1] No sooner had we anchored than several boatloads of people came out to look at us. We seemed to puzzle them greatly. The Harbour-master came on board, and took our name, etc., for the local newspaper. As we were tired after our passage from Stornoway, 214 miles, we did not land, but had supper, and turned in.

Next morning, before breakfast, we were hailed, and a man in a boat presented us with a *Memento of Faeroe*, a local sketch in oils, painted by himself. It was a charming little picture, and has a place of honour in *Emanuel*'s cabin. Our visitor's name was Sigmund Petersen. We saw more of him later.

[1] Later we found these were heaps of partially dried fish.

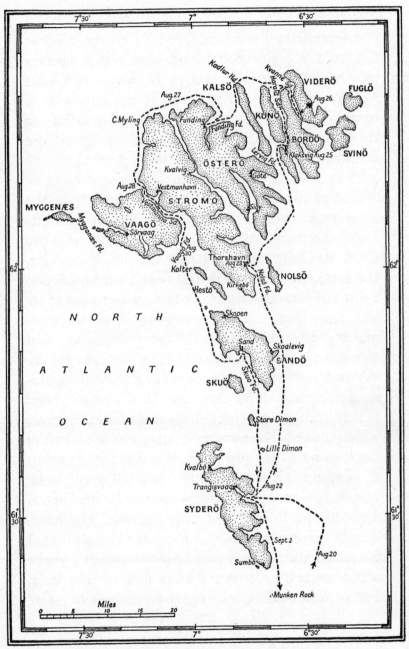

THE FAEROE ISLANDS

In my diary I see I recorded: 'This morning so far (11 a.m.) nine boats have been out to see us, mostly manned by small boys, but one was a boat-load of girls, obviously brought out specially to examine us. Apparently the boys may come by themselves, but the girls must be brought.' We went ashore about noon, and were greeted on the jetty by crowds of small children, who gazed at us with rapt attention. We felt a little embarrassed at so much attention, though later we got used to it.

A fisherman told one of the boys to take us to the Customs Office, and the larger and bolder boys led the way, the rest following. Thus we proceeded to the Harbourmaster's office, surrounded by children—quite a royal procession. The Harbour-master, Mr. Hansen, was very amiable, and directed us to the hotel, where we ordered lunch. We had not been long enough in Faeroe to appreciate the meal. The soup was thick with grease. It was brought in with the meat, so that the meat, which looked like lumps of mud, was cold by the time we were ready to eat it. It was boiled mutton, and came from Little Dimon, a small precipitous island; climbing the rocky slopes of Little Dimon evidently made strong, sturdy animals. The land-lady thought one krone each (about two shillings) too much, but we persuaded her to take that, so she compromised by making me a pair of sheepskin Faeroe shoes. They all wear these skin shoes. The girls have red strings attached, and the boys and men white. Some men wear heavier cowhide shoes.

The men still wear their national dress, which consists of breeches, tight about the knees, fastened by a number of silver buttons, and a loose, natural brown coat with more buttons down the front. Their stockings and coats are usually home spun and woven. Their hat is a curious-shaped cap affair, which is striped, either narrow white and blue, or red, white, and blue. The girls wear ordinary, modern clothing. The language is their own. It came from an old Norse dialect, and has only recently been reproduced in writing.

Old Mr. and Mrs. Petersen could not write Faeroese, but, of course, they could speak it, and write Danish. Danish is the official language. At school they now learn Danish, Faeroese, and English. Nearly everyone speaks a little English, picked up chiefly from trawlers that stop there on their way to Iceland. We had no difficulty in making ourselves understood.

After lunch we walked out to the end of the fiord, where we had a magnificent view. There were telegraph wires all along the road, a glorified path, and quite impossible to wheeled traffic, which was lit by electric lamps. We saw a number of men in their national dress, cutting their tiny patches of hay. They used scythes with a very short, straight blade. The hay, which grew in spots wherever the land permitted it, should have been cut some time ago. We also passed a few very minute, unique patches of corn. The cows must live a lonely life, for they are kept tethered to the wayside, and not allowed to roam. If they were, they would probably fall over the cliff. What struck us was the contrast between old and new—electric light and telegraph poles along the road, yet all the road transport done on foot, except for an occasional bicycle; the old men in their national dress, with the girls in their silk stockings and fur-necked coats. Inside the cottages one would see a woman spinning with a telephone at her elbow.

Coming home we met Mr. Petersen, who asked us to come to his house in the evening. We were not quite sure whether he meant to supper or not. I thought he said something about food, but skipper was uncertain. We were starving after our walk, but only had a light meal in case we were to eat at the Petersens'. I was right, we did have a meal. The food was infinitely superior to that of the hotel. I was rather stumped, as I didn't know if we were meant to use the same plate all the time; apparently we were.

Old Mr. and Mrs. Petersen were charming. They had extraordinarily kind faces. The family consisted of Mr. and Mrs. Petersen, Sigmund, Thorolo, a cousin, and two girl cousins, Lula and

Joanna. The girls had their meals in the kitchen, and joined the rest afterwards. Sigmund and Mr. Petersen could talk quite good English, Mrs. Petersen a little, and the others none. When we were just about to go, about 9.30, we were given some delicious pineapple and cream. All the younger members of the family accompanied us back to *Emanuel*, where we gave them beer. They admired *Emanuel* very much.

After breakfast next day, Sigmund came off and asked if we would take him with us to Thorshavn, and we agreed. The wind was very squally, so we only had storm jib, reefed mainsail, and foresail set. Outside the sea was steep and irregular. The cliffs were magnificent, nearly all rising sheer out of the water to a great height. As we neared Thorshavn we passed a couple of little open Viking boats, as we called them, on account of their shape, which resembled the Viking ships of old.[1] They were really a lovely sight, plunging against a head sea. They would rear up on the crest of a wave, half the boat being out of water, and then crash down again with a terrific splash, yet not a drop

[1] A typical Faeroe boat is twenty-one feet overall, and has six feet beam, the shape being that of the old Viking ships. The oars are peculiar, the blade being only two and a half inches wide. The loom is fitted with an elaborately shaped piece of oak, which takes a strop to secure the oar to the thole pin. They are now nearly all fitted with engines, but we saw several sailing with a small sprit mainsail and foresail.

came on board. There was only one man in each boat, and he was as bold and cheery as you like. One knew Sigmund, and they hailed each other gaily. It was an exhilarating sight.

We reached Thorshavn in the afternoon. It is the capital, and much larger than Trangisvaag, being more of a town. There are even a few cars there. We landed before a crowd of astonished children, and one boy took us up to the hotel; this boy had learnt English at school, and could speak it quite well. He seemed glad to have an opportunity of airing his knowledge. Sigmund gave us dinner. We had liver, one of my pet abominations. There was a melon on the table, and skipper loves melon; every now and then his gaze wandered towards it, but it never came to us, alas! After dinner Sigmund took us for a walk round the town. In one shop were some pictures he had painted. They were exceedingly good: he is an artist. He taught himself, and I am sure he would be famous had he been to an art school in Europe.

Next morning we called at the British Consulate, but the Consul was away on holiday. Sigmund took us to a house where they sold hand-knitted jerseys and socks, and after buying a jersey, we were invited to partake of tea and cakes with the family. We lunched at the sailors' home, and found it a much better place than the hotel. There was one old man who asked numerous questions about

Emanuel and her voyage, replying to each answer, 'That's good.' He seemed to understand.

After lunch we were taken in a Chevrolet to Kirkebö, a large farm. It had once been the largest town in Faeroe, but an avalanche had pushed all the houses into the sea. There was no loss of life, though, for the people were all in the church, which withstood the snow. The drive was rather nerve-racking, for the road was very stony and narrow. Periodically there were hairpin bends and right-angled turns, while all the way there was the steep hill-side, and the fiord below looking ready to receive us if our driver should swerve too much. It was very squally, and down in the fiord we could see little whirlwinds lashing up the apparently smooth water. We could also see several British trawlers coming into Thorshavn for shelter. We arrived at Kirkebö without mishap, and were shown the remains of an old church, which was never finished. The Bishop who was building it, so legend says, fell into disfavour with the natives, who tried to kill him. He escaped to the top of the wall by means of a secret passage, and remained there for three days. The strain proved too much for him, so he fell off, and was torn to pieces by the mob below.

The farm-house is a fascinating place. It is built on a foundation of stone, in which was an old dungeon. The top was of old wooden logs, which they assured us were nine hundred years old. Entering the living-room one felt as if one had entered a large farm-house or manor in England, several hundred years ago. The walls were plain, and of wood; at one end there were whaling spears, all greased and ready for use, hung on the wall. In another corner was a stone quern. Down the middle of the room was a wooden table, with bare wooden benches round it. Mr. Patursen, the owner of this farm, is one of the chief Faeroemen. He is their representative in the Danish Parliament and leader of the Home Rule party. What made our visit to the village so pleasant was that we were treated as guests, and not as tourists. From no house that we visited in the whole Islands were we ever allowed to go without first having partaken of some refreshment, usually tea and cakes. There was a large garden at Kirkebö, too, the largest in the Islands. There were a few strawberries in it, and our guide offered us some. Skipper, having picked several tons of strawberries earlier in the season, was very *blasé* about them, and refused. However, we were pressed to try them, and he consented, much to my relief. I am not so *blasé* about strawberries, for I am never at home during the season. We were shown a spinning-wheel, too, and I was allowed to try my hand on it. It looked very easy, but I was singularly unsuccessful.

We dined at the sailors' home, where we met

three Englishmen who had been fishing. They were going home by the mail boat that evening. Next morning, the 24th, we were under way about 11. We dipped to a Danish man-of-war, which was very smart in answering our salute. We had a glorious sail to Klaksvig. The sun came out for the first part, and the cliffs are wonderful at the entrance to Lervig Sound. Looking through the Sound, it appears to be an avenue of great, purple pyramids, their colour becoming bluer as they fade away into the distance. We had to beat through the Sound, and presently it came on to blow, but the water was smooth. It was very exhilarating struggling with the helm and sheets. We gybed as we entered Klaksvig fiord, and the main sheet, on which I was pulling with all my strength, took charge, and ran out, leaving a red line down my leg where it rubbed. Just as we anchored it poured with rain, so we were drenched, but the cabin felt all the more cosy and quiet afterwards.

The next day was a Sunday. After lunch we went ashore for a walk. We climbed up part of a mountain, about 1,000 feet, and skipper got quite excited, for we found some plants that were of an Arctic type. The hill-side was very boggy and wet, and there were numbers of waterfalls and torrents tearing down it. I was more comfortable in my bare legs and sandshoes than skipper in his socks and boots, which got very wet. When we came back we went to the Hotel British, and asked for tea. This was about 4.30. After the proprietress of the hotel had told us all her family history, and mistaken me for a girl of twelve or thirteen,[1] though before they thought I was skipper's wife, we were provided with a sort of high tea, with lots of dried meat. The meat must have been a very long time drying; it was rather strong to our English taste. The old lady said she liked the English. She had met a great number of sailors from British trawlers, 'But,' she said, 'I haf neveer meet one bad Engleeshman, and so I call my place Hotel British.' [2]

It made us rather proud to feel that we, too, were British. She flatly refused to let us pay for our meal, and gave us milk as well. Where in England, I wonder, would a hotel refuse payment for a meal? As we went back the end of skipper's pipe fell off, and he turned rather sharply to pick it up. His movement frightened the crowd of children who were following, and they turned and fled. However, when they discovered he meant no harm, and only wanted his pipe, they were very amused. Skipper rashly said that anyone who liked might come on board. There was great

[1] Mate was aged seventeen.
[2] The landlady told us she had watched us entering. When we gybed she had turned away from the window as she could not bear to see us drown! There was no danger really.

excitement, and crowds came off in boats. At one time there were so many on the stern that the water started coming up through the cockpit drain hole. The first people had cake, but that ran out at No. 30. Yet still more came. Altogether seventy-one people, of all ages and sexes, came aboard. A number of small boys came twice. Rather an exhausting evening.

We left Klaksvig about 8.30 next day, and had a delightful sail through Harald fiord, anchoring near the Narrows in Kvanne Sund.[1] We went ashore and examined a derelict whaling station. There was not much to be seen, only a few bones. We left Kvanne Sund in the afternoon, and spent the evening becalmed off the entrance. The cliffs and hills were magnificent, and in the distance we could see Cape Myling, some sixteen miles off, looking about eight miles away. We saw Fuglö behind Viderö, so we had seen both the most Northern and most Western extremities of the Islands. Gradually, with the help of occasional puffs of wind and the tide, we drifted along past Kadlur Head, making for Funding fiord, which we reached in the early hours of the morning.

Next day we were again becalmed off the mouth of the fiord, but later picked up enough wind to

[1] Three sets of iron beacons lead through the Narrows, but are not marked on the chart. This was the first day of our cruise without some rain.

take us down to Cape Myling, where we again lost the wind.[1] Cape Myling is a magnificent cliff. It rises nearly 2,000 feet, sheer out of the sea. At its feet are rocky caves and projections. We were very much impressed by its imposing grandeur. We gradually made our way down to Vestmanna Sund, where we found a fresh, squally breeze that took us up to Vestmanhavn, where we anchored, had supper, and went to bed.

We went ashore after breakfast next morning, and bought some badly needed bread. We had been living on ship's biscuits for the last few days. We were unable to get butter here. Then we called on a trawler, the *St. Endellion*, to ask for a chronometer comparison, our usual excuse. We were entertained in the captain's cabin, under the bridge, where there were several other trawler skippers. A girl seemed a bit out of place, but they were all very friendly. The ship was extraordinarily well fitted out and clean. The skipper, Captain McGreggor, was a naturalised British subject, having been Russian, from Riga, before the war. We had tea on board, an enormous meal, and afterwards Captain McGreggor, or Russian George, as he was nicknamed, told us thrilling

---

[1] 1.30 P.M., tide race of Kadlur (Osterö), strong wind, and nasty sea; stowed jib and put three rolls in mainsail, when yacht became more manageable. Mate had to exert all her strength at the tiller.

stories of Russia before the War. His brother had been sentenced to twenty years in Siberia, but had been released when the war came, after ten years. He himself had run away to sea. After serving in Russian ships he came to the conclusion that British sailors had a better time than Russians, and he joined the British Merchant Service. He told us how one day some Cossacks came into the schoolroom, and asked questions, emphasising each question with a flick of their whips on the desks. Afterwards they saw the whips had made cuts in the wood a quarter of an inch deep.

The weather was too bad for sailing that evening, so we remained in the harbour. Mr. Sam Olsen took us up to an inland lake next morning. We had an exhilarating climb up. It was blowing hard, and raining, but it was energetic work walking, and we kept warm. When we arrived we had to wait about and watch Mr. Olsen wading knee-deep in icy-cold water. That alone was enough to make anyone feel cold, but the wind and rain nearly turned us into icicles. However, we managed to keep our circulation going by running mad races, which had no beginnings or ends. We only caught one fish, as it was blowing so hard.[1] Mr. Olsen gave us coffee and cakes when we returned, and then we went on board again, and changed into dry clothes. The Faeroe jerseys

[1] We saw some specimens of the Arctic hare among the rocks.

are wonderful garments. I was wearing one, with no coat or mackintosh, yet in spite of continuous rain all the morning I was quite dry underneath it.

In the evening we went on board the *Islands Falk*, a Danish gunboat, to buy some butter. We were given some, but not allowed to pay for it. The officers were very friendly, and all spoke very good English. They gave us a weather report, and also a news bulletin. From that we learnt there had been trouble in Palestine some weeks ago.

We got under way next morning, but were becalmed most of the day. There were a number of small Faeroe boats about catching birds.[1] They just motored up to a bird which was sitting on the water, and fished it up in a net. Why the idiotic birds did not get out of the way is beyond my comprehension. One boat came up to us, and offered us a bird—but, 'No, thanks!' There was a mass of quivering white feathers in the bottom, enough to put anyone off. We passed the Troll's Finger. It was a very fine needle rock, and Sigmund had told us the legend about it, but we never quite understood the story. It had some connection with a wicked witch who harmed sailors. The breeze was so light that we decided to go into Sandvaag; as it grew dusk the breeze freshened, and when I came up on deck we were close to the shore, with a line of breakers almost under us. We went about, and

[1] Fulmar.

crossed over to the other shore, which was also very noisy and alarming, so we turned round and fled for Trangisvaag. By 2.30 a.m. we were just off the entrance, and at 3.30 we anchored, and turned in.

After breakfast, at 9.30, the Petersens came off, and invited us to lunch. We showed the old people over the ship, and they seemed very interested. After lunch we got under way and, accompanied by a large proportion of the population in boats, sailed down the fiord, dipping on the way to *Islands Falk*. Outside we had a strong breeze and horrible rain. The glass started to fall sharply, and after a few hours skipper decided things were not good enough for making a passage, so we turned back and re-anchored in Trangisvaag. The next day, Sunday, 1st September, the Petersens took us fishing. It did not rain at first, but, of course, poured later. There was a thick fog, and we could see nothing, but the Petersens seemed to know the way. The roads, or rather the best way across the mountains, for there are no roads, are marked by cairns. There is a very real danger of losing oneself in the fog on the hills. When we arrived at the lake one of the boys lent me a pair of waders, for which I was very grateful. They offered skipper a pair, but being a man he refused, as one of them would have had to go without. Not being a man, I did not refuse. We fished with worms, not, I believe, the correct thing, but we caught dozens. Skipper caught the first, but I caught the biggest. I caught four altogether. It was great fun, but rather cold and damp. We climbed home, and after changing on board, returned to the Petersens for supper. We had an excellent meal. They had killed a chicken specially for us, knowing we did not appreciate the usual dried meat, or boiled mutton. Mr. Petersen and one of the boys stayed behind to catch some more fish, but they missed their way, and were very late returning. After supper they sang old Faeroe folk songs. Some were very charming, and full of expression.

We left Faeröerne on Monday. Sigmund and Thorolo came off in the morning with milk and cakes, and also our clothes, which they had very kindly dried for us. Some days later, when putting on a clean blouse, I discovered a piece of paper in the pocket, signed 'Thorolo,' and bearing these words on it: 'ei kán laik ju veni ves.' Can anyone translate it for me? No one that I have met so far can, so I am still ignorant of its meaning, and should be interested to find it out. We again dipped to the *Islands Falk*, and s.s. *Emerald* hooted to us, so we replied with our little tin whistle of a foghorn. It was quite a spectacular exit. We were accompanied to the mouth of the fiord by a number of small rowing- and motor-boats. We had a grand sail outside, making six knots with a reefed mainsail. Gradually the Faeroes receded into the distance, till eventually we lost sight of them. Adieu, Faeroe! We had a very jolly fortnight sailing among the 'little rock Islands of the Atlantic,' as Sigmund so aptly described his home, and we were sorry to see the last of them.

After we had run seventy-four and a quarter miles in twelve hours[1] the wind got tired, and went light. We spent most of Tuesday becalmed. In the morning we both turned in. About 11 we were startled to hear a siren hooting outside. On turning out to investigate we found a trawler, which presumably had come to see what a yacht was doing with no one at the helm. About 5 P.M. a breeze deigned to come, and took us in sight of North Rona; but the effort was too much for it, and it went again, leaving us without steerage way. We therefore turned in with a riding light up.

[1] It may be of interest to compare this with the first *Tern*'s best run of 62 miles in 10 hr. 25 min. (*Yacht Cruising*, by C. Worth, 3rd Ed., p. 70). *Tern* was 3 ft. 6 in. longer on the W.L., 10 in. narrower, and 1 ft. deeper than *Emanuel*. She had a crew of three able-bodied men, and was evidently being driven with her lee rail awash. *Emanuel* was running under comparatively easy sail. My rough log contains the statement that reefs were needed, which was true enough. With only two on board long spells at the helm are necessary, and one cannot steer with that care which would be possible if a third hand were available. Also, it is advisable to shorten sail, before that operation becomes difficult.

Worth's formula for maximum sustained speed works out at seven knots for *Emanuel*. We have not reached this, but have never really driven her yet.

Early next morning we had a breeze, which took us to Stornoway, where we anchored at about 10.15 P.M.

We were under way next day at 2.30 A.M., and reached South Rona. Then the wind left us, and we spent another night becalmed. However, a breeze sprang up next morning, and we had a delightful sail through Kyle Akin, the inner passage between Skye and the Mainland. We anchored for the night in Loch Beiste, a beautiful little loch, the woods coming right down to the water's edge. We were much impressed with the beauty of these Scotch lochs and highlands, but it is quite beyond my powers to attempt to describe them.

Next day, Saturday, 7th September, was very thick, and we only had a light head wind. We got down the Sound of Sleat to Dun Bane, where we anchored for a tide. Sunday was a repetition of Saturday, fog and head wind, but we managed to get as far as the Island of Eigg. Next morning we saw two yachts outside, so got under way full speed, and tried to catch them up. We hoisted our topsail, and started catching up one, a black yawl, but then she hoisted her balloon foresail, and ran away from us. The other yacht, also a yawl, stood farther out. We cut off a corner rounding Ardnamurcha, and by the time we reached Oban she was hull down behind us. We spent Tuesday at Oban, and on Wednesday got down to Scarba

Island. We rounded Kintyre on Thursday evening.

On Friday it was obvious skipper had a rotten cold, so we went into Peel, in the Isle of Man.[1] Saturday was a day in harbour, skipper's cold still being nasty. We left Peel on Sunday, and spent the next few days with hardly any wind. By Tuesday afternoon we had reached the Bishop, but were almost becalmed. When I turned out on Wednesday morning we were abeam of St. Anne's Lighthouse, and St. Gowan's lightship was ahead. We then had a wonderful sail. It was very thrilling speeding up Channel with a fair breeze, and all sail set, picking up the old familiar headlands as we went. As we neared Minehead the great question was, 'Could we catch the tide into Burnham, and up to Bridgwater?' We rushed through the water, a frantic race against time, but we won! We caught the tide just in time to sail up the Parret.

We were excited when we dropped anchor outside the dock gates, yet as we were towed through the gates into the docks we were sorry that *Emanuel* would not feel the 'wash and thresh of the sea foam' about her bows for another year. She had given us a very jolly cruise indeed.

[1] Skipper was very seedy all day, leaving the mate to steer, and do all the work.

ADVENTURE OF THE FAEROE ISLANDS

			Miles
Aug.	1.	River Parrett	$\frac{1}{2}$
„	2.	R. Parrett to Minehead	29
„	3.	Minehead to Ilfracombe	25
„	4.	Ilfracombe to Oxwich B.	20
„	5.	Oxwich B. to Caldy I. and Tenby	24
„	6.	Tenby to Ramsey Sound	37
„	7.	Ramsey Sound to Fishguard	20
„	8–10.	Fishguard to Donaghadee	160
„	11–12.	Donaghadee to L. Don	114
„	12.	L. Don to Ardtonish B.	8
„	13–14.	Ardtonish B. to Stornoway	125
„	15.	At Stornoway	—
„	16.	Stornoway to L. Erisort and back (sailed)	16
„	17.	At Stornoway	—
„	18–20.	Stornoway to Trangisvaag	214
„	21.	At Trangisvaag	—
„	22.	Trangisvaag to Thorshavn	33
„	23.	At Thorshavn	—
„	24.	Thorshavn to Klaksvig	18
„	25.	At Klaksvig	—
„	26.	Klaksvig to Kvanne Sand and Funding	31
„	27.	Funding to Vestmanhavn	25
„	28–29.	At Vestmanhavn	—
„	30.	Vestmanhavn to Sand and Trangisvaag	48
„	31.	At Trangisvaag (sailed)	10
Sept.	1.	At Trangisvaag	—
„	2–4.	Trangisvaag to Stornoway	214
„	5–6.	Stornoway to L. Beiste	65
„	7.	L. Beiste to Dun Bane	16
„	8.	Dun Bane to Eigg I.	16
„	9.	Eigg I. to Oban	42
„	10.	At Oban	—
„	11.	Oban to Scarba Sound	17
„	12–13.	Scarba Sound to Peel (I. of Man)	130
„	14.	At Peel	—
„	15–18.	Peel to Bridgwater	261

$$1,718\frac{1}{2}$$